the Bible makes Sense

revised edition

the Bible makes Sense

revised edition

Walter Brueggemann

ST. ANTHONY MESSENGER PRESS

Cincinnati, Ohio

Cover design by Mike Winegardner

ISBN-13: 978-0-86716-558-6
ISBN-10: 0-86716-558-8

Copyright © 2003, Walter Brueggemann. All rights reserved.
Published by St. Anthony Messenger Press
28 W. Liberty St.
Cincinnati, OH 45202
www.SAMPBooks.org

Printed in the United States of America
Printed on acid-free paper

11 12 7 6 5 4

Contents

Foreword

This is a "how to" book of an unusual kind. The author proposes that Christians should approach the Bible, not as a collection of ancient documents, but as our partner in an ongoing dialog about our life here and now. He explains how to enter into this dialog, how to listen, and how to respond. Suggestions for reflection, discussion, and meditation on particular passages provide outlines for group study and for the individual reader's own prayerful Bible reading.

Thus the book is not meant to be one more introduction to the Bible, or commentary on it, giving historical or literary information—useful as these are. It is about the Christian way of approaching the Bible as the life-giving word of God addressed to us. It has, then, much to offer both to those entrusted with proclaiming this word to a Christian community as preachers and to all of us who are called to live by it and proclaim it in our life and actions.

Mary Perkins Ryan
Editor

1

The Possibility
of a Fresh Perspective

It is strange that the Bible is our most treasured book, and yet it seems so difficult that we don't find it very helpful. Perhaps we have expected the wrong things of it; we have asked of it what it cannot do. We have expected the Bible to keep promises that it has never made to us. The Bible cannot be a good luck piece to bring God's blessing. Nor can it be an answer book to solve our problems or to give us right belief. So the first question about reading the Bible is what we can indeed expect of it.

I suggest that the Bible is precious to us because it offers us a way of understanding the world in a fresh perspective, a perspective that leads to life, joy, and wholeness. It offers us a model, a pattern, through which we may think about, perceive, and live life differently. Each of us has adopted one or more models for living, even though we didn't do it consciously. We learned a certain perspective by living in certain contexts and listening to certain voices. Those might have been the voices of fearful parents or of calculating peers. They might have been the voices of grudging tradition or euphoric dreams. Among the voices many of us listened to were the smooth seductive voices of television commercials. Each of these voices shaped our consciousness and urged us to a particular notion of life. They gripped our life and shaped our experience, and we didn't know it was happening. Yet over a period of time, they came to have great power over us and finally to define our identity and destiny.

The model that I regard as central to the Bible and that I will present here is what I call a *covenantal-historical* way of understanding our life and faith. By *covenantal* I mean an enduring commitment between God and God's people based on mutual vows of loyalty and mutual obligation through which both parties have their life radically affected and empowered. By *historical* I mean that these covenant partners, God and God's people, have a vast deposit of precious memories of decisive interactions. These interactions, which run the gamut of love and hate, affirm to us that our whole existence depends on staying seriously and faithfully involved with the covenant partner, even at some risk.

To bring out the uniqueness of this covenantal-historical model, I will first sketch out several models, or ways of understanding life, that are shaping people in our society. In some respects, they have points of contact with the model here proposed and are reflected in the Bible. But on the whole it is clear, as I will try to show, that the biblical view is quite distinctive from the others. The reading of the Bible can offer to us ways of understanding our life that are quite different from our own ways and perhaps even in contradiction. Exposure to this literature may challenge our imagination and present to us ways of thinking and perceiving and knowing that have been denied to us by other lenses of perception.

The Modern-Industrial-Scientific Model

The modern-industrial-scientific model of understanding the world has emerged in the last several centuries and has been of decisive importance in shaping our public institutions. It includes the notion that knowledge is power and, therefore, that life consists in acquiring enough knowledge to control and predict our world, and thereby to secure our life against every danger and threat.

This model also includes the notion that life is built on a reliable scheme of performance and reward. Put in traditional language, "Good people prosper, evil people suffer." Put in more contemporary language, it means that everyone and everything is valued for his or her usefulness. Life is governed by a firm arrangement of effectiveness and payoffs, whether in the marketplace, the home, or the church. All relations take on a quid pro quo pattern. Such an understanding of reality places a high value on competence and achieving, on success and getting ahead. Such a view yields a notion of personhood that says, "I have value for what I do," or in its more decadent form, "I have value for what I have." The human community consists of people getting what they earn and deserve. Those who earn little and therefore deserve little do not figure; in fact, for practical purposes they do not even exist. Obviously, such a view favors those who succeed and are competent. It tends to be the case that those who have, get more, and those who don't have, get less or nothing.

This model applies to kids in the Little League who never get to play as well as to the poor who never share in the riches of society. Such a model of course destroys those who are left out. But it also destroys those who benefit, for finally no one can succeed enough, and so everyone is too anxious and too driven and finally alienated. This model, which lies at the heart of the American perception of reality and which shapes most of our institutions, clearly resists the good news of the Gospel, for it is based on the assumption that graciousness must be banished.

As a result, this view puts a premium on what is knowable, manageable, and predictable. Clearly it does not appreciate graciousness, for everything is earned. It is not open to mystery, for everything must be explained. It has no space for transcendence, because everything must be managed. While much of our modern world is organized this way, and many of us are deeply into it when we least know it, such a model of reality is quite at variance with that of the Bible.

The Existentialist Model

Persons who have found the modern model wanting, have looked for an alternative. And they have found one. They have wanted an alternative to a world that is rational and objective and so have fashioned a model of reality that in some ways is the very opposite of the modern-industrial-scientific model. If we cannot live life by what we know in a cool way, perhaps we can live by the hot action of making decisions.

Existentialism has many popular forms. An existentialist can be the loner "who must do his own thing" and who believes it morally irresponsible to rely on tradition, on long-standing communities, and on institutions. An existentialist feels that a community is by definition an act of deception or bad faith, and finally the individual person must live his or her own life by his or her own resources. This model tends to be evident among young persons who must leave home, among rebels who believe that all rules must be broken and all seasoned decisions rejected.

This perspective was originally articulated to present an alternative to a coldly objective and rational world of control and mastery. Existentialism holds that meaning exists only in, and derives from, the decisions made by the individual in the present moment. It is thus a protest, and an important one, against a static view of reality that regards everything as fixed and closed and insists on keeping it that way. Conversely, this model of reality tends to be community-denying, locating meaning only in terms of the solitary decision maker, who must not only make decisions alone but also live with the consequences.

Along with such uncompromising individualism, this model also tends to devalue the historical process as it moves from event to event. It finds no meaning in the sweep of history or in the continuities of the process because meaning is located only in the *now* of the present decision. While this view does appreciate the full power of the present moment, it tends to leave the individual in a vacuum because, by definition, memories and hopes are not matters of significance for the identity or destiny of the individual.

In brief, existentialism posits the human decision maker as the sole agent of meaning. Not only can meanings not be appropriated from others, there is no possibility of transcendent meaning in experience. No meanings can be given to, or be prior to, the individual in the moment. While existentialism intends to be a statement of radical freedom and responsibility, it also holds the likely prospect of weariness and despair. While the promise is great, if my world depends solely on me, that is more than I can bear.

The Transcendentalist Model

The transcendentalist view of reality is for those who believe that life is too complicated to endure and too messy to be the place of meaning. And so they believe there is another sphere of reality that is simple, clear, unsoiled, and uncomplicated. The real meanings do not emerge from the power struggles in our life, even in our love relationships, but must be found in a sphere protected from all of that. This model appears in the romantic notions of love and marriage in much of the American dream that envisions a "little home in love land," where we won't have a telephone, that is, we won't be bothered by reality. But it also has its religious forms, in which pious language and stained-glass windows pretend to screen out the cries of hunger and the groans of injustice. Enduring meaning is immune from the incongruities and discontinuities of historical experience and may be located beyond historical experience in an abiding and enduring state of eternity.

Such a history-denying view of life has a variety of manifestations. It may be expressed as cold reason that regards only logic as providing relevant data. Conversely, it may be mystical meditation that seeks to negate historical experience, to be emptied of such sensitivities for the sake of other once-removed meanings. Such a quest for nonhistorical reality may be pursued by meditative reflection after the manner of Eastern religions or, more broadly, in religious celebrations that serve to escape the realities of daily life.

Transcendentalism tends to deny suffering and to seek serenity beyond the reaches of historical hurt. Implicit in such a view is the conviction that historical experience and indeed historical personality are not essential embodiments of fundamental meaning. It will be evident that such a view of religion is in conflict with a religion of incarnation, that is, of historical embodiment of decisive meaning. Transcendentalism tends to deny the exigencies of historical risk and hurt. It imagines that life can be lived without involvement with unattractive persons. It pretends that life can be an uninterrupted tranquillity without any abrasions. It conjures a God who dwells in a quiet heaven to sanction such a settled life. It is finally in conflict with the religion of Jesus, who knew that the power of God is shown precisely where there are hurting, sick, lame people. And so even among people who are in every way sophisticated and concerned with the mastery of their lives, some are tempted to an unthinking religion in which responsibility dissolves and one can embrace an undifferentiated experience of good feeling in which persons can abdicate, make no decisions, or take any responsibility.

None of us, obviously, ever embodies any of these models fully or intentionally. But they do exercise great influence in the shaping of personality and in defining cultural values and expectations. It is clear that we never perceive any of them fully and consistently, but only in hints and tendencies. Thus the *modern-industrial-scientific* view probably prevails in our public institutions, such as schools and hospitals, and certainly dominates the job market, which pays primary attention to competence and performance for the sake of profit. To be sure, there are always dimensions of compassion and grace, but they do not make a decisive difference.

Again, *existentialism* will not often surface among us in pure form, but it molds much of counter-culture life and has an important appeal for some of the young. It is perhaps the vision of youth that all worlds are possible and any is choosable. And *transcendentalism* is often proper religion that is just now surfacing, especially among respectable dropouts of the modern-industrial-scientific view of life, which has not kept its promises. The discovery of these unkept promises invites people to withdraw to "religion."

The Covenantal-Historical Model

The covenantal-historical model may be contrasted at important points with the "different faith models" we have already reviewed. Distinct from the *modern-industrial-scientific* view, covenantal-historical faith affirms that human existence does not consist primarily in the capacity to know and control and manage. Against a this-for-that world based on success and competence, it asserts that real life with God consists in risking commitments, in powerful memories, and compelling visions. Distinct from *existentialism,* this perspective asserts that meanings are never private but always communal, never to be found in an isolated "now," but always in an ongoing process of trust and betrayal, and never with individual persons as the only actors. It insists that life consists in a dialog with a powerful, compelling Other who bestows mercy and compels accountability. The God whom we confess is a serious partner in our life. We may pray to God for mercy because God does not give us what we have coming to us. God does not settle for quid pro quo. God does not deal with us according to our iniquities, but does take our loyalty seriously. God leaves us not free but requires that our life be lived in answer to God's expectations. In both God's mercy and expectations, it means we are being taken with ultimate seriousness. Distinct from *transcendentalism,* the biblical frame of reference denies that meaning can be immune from the incongruities and discontinuities of history. These discontinuities include such things as the real grief of death that cannot be explained as a "growth point," the real failures of relationships, the real collapse of institutions upon which we have relied. It asserts that decisive meanings are located in and derived precisely from historical hurts and historical amazements that judge and heal and call to repentance.

When we read the Bible, then, we need to learn to pay attention to the understandings of reality that permeate the text. Unless we do this, we may fail to discern what is in fact present to the text and to the church. For the believing community is always confronted by the text as summoning it to make a new decision about perspective.

Thus one main reason why we read Scripture is so that we may not settle easily for any other notion of life, forgetting who we are and the understanding of life that we have confessed and embraced. Informed by the Bible, we are invited to live in faithful response to this faithful covenant partner. Such a possibility is not guaranteed by Scripture study, but it is peculiar to our faith tradition and provides us with a context for living quite different from the reigning alternatives. In other words, one of the most important gifts the Bible can give us is a frame of reference for our life. Given that frame of reference, we are still left with major decisions to make about our world, our freedom, and our responsibility. But Scripture reading can provide us with resources and images enabling us to understand, embrace, and respond to life in all its richness. For the Bible presents human life in terms of the vitality of being in history with a covenantal partner who speaks newness in a world that always seems fatigued and exhausted. That is what is most deeply characteristic about this view of reality: that we are in covenant with One who speaks newness, who dismantles what is old in our life, and who calls us to welcome and live toward newness.

From the viewpoint of the alternatives, the Bible presents a curious reading of reality quite out of harmony with that proposed by other viewpoints. Of course the elements about which we are speaking are nowhere neatly spelled out in systematic fashion. But they do emerge, and their emergence in diverse times and places is important as resource and context for all of us in the church. Four dimensions of covenant summarized below are especially important as they hint of a new history in which we might live.

Some Characteristics of the Biblical View

1. Biblical faith is not interested in the kind of general religious or moral questions that might interest us. It is always intently concerned for *concreteness,* both in terms of what is expected in human behavior and in terms of what God is doing. Thus, Jesus had no general theory of healing, but he healed persons and condemned institutions that worked against healing. In the Hebrew Scriptures, God's will for justice is always embodied in concrete acts of power and mercy.

This idea of covenant affirms that a particular people are peculiarly bearers of a promise that has a high degree of specificity. On the one hand, this particularity is an embarrassment because it sounds quite unsophisticated to locate primary meanings in historical happenings. On the other hand, it is precisely

identity in a particular community (Israel, the church) that en-
ergizes and authorizes a clear identity and a bold mission. This
community—that is, the people especially in covenant with the
Lord, the God of the Bible—is bound to God in loyalty and
obedience. It concerns not just anyone anywhere but is a locat-
able community. This characteristic is crucial in a culture in
which many people experience displacement. Thus God's special and specific work is to call a distinct people in the historical process to do God's work and trust God's promises. A
Bible-reading church is not free to deny these peculiar marks of
identity and burden.

2. Covenantal-historical perspectives help people claim
precise historical memory. We do not live in an abstract realm
of ideas, but in a people that has a particular memory that
gives power to us. People do not derive strength or energy by
belonging to a general diffuse collection of people. Rather they
have their identity by membership in an identifiable community with a history and a vision. In our situation, the re-emergence
of ethnic consciousness as well as churches facing new questions of discipline are parts of the urgency of particularity in
our humanness. Memory, as it is expressed in biblical faith, is a
memory of historical liberation (Exodus) and empowerment
(David), of passionate caring-suffering (crucifixion) and the surprise of new life (resurrection).

This rootage tells us something about God, that God is not
a remote, self-serving agent who is for God alone; God is for
us, characteristically involved on behalf of all creatures. On the
one hand, our life is not about private matters, so that success-
es or failures or hurt or well-being are just mine. On the other
hand, our life is not about sweeping generalizations. Rather our
life, as we remember and retell it, is about all our experiences
set in a concrete community that preserves the memories and
keeps returning to them to draw power and authority for living.
It is about liberation and empowerment, about self-giving for
others, and about being surprised by new life when we thought
it not possible. Our identity is secured in the places of cost and
joy in which we have been involved. It is this very particular
memory to which we are heirs and of which we are bearers.
And when we ask who we are, we answer in terms of these

events that have happened in our common past and that continue to happen in our common life. For those who have eyes to discern, the Bible is the account of this very special history that lies behind and helps shape our present attitudes toward life and faith. The vision and promise of the Bible cannot easily be adapted to the way things presently are. Indeed there is some incompatibility between that vision of justice and our present society, between that promise of peace and the way things now are. And as the community of the Bible embraces the vision of the future, it must increasingly be in tension with present arrangements and open to radical changes as God's promises come among us.

3. A fresh perspective of a covenantal-historical kind transmits to us a *special expectation for the future and a dynamic that lets that promised future come among us*. The shape of our expectation is quite concrete even though it tends to be expressed in poetic imagery. We live toward and await the coming of a community of justice and righteousness, in which the last ones will be first (Luke 13:30), in which the humbled ones will be exalted (Luke 14:11), in which the hungry ones will be fed (Luke 1:53), and in which the ones who mourn will be comforted (Matt. 5:4). Our expected future, which God has promised in the Bible, has many points of commonality with the best of civil religion and with the substance of the American dream. But the texture of this future is expressed in the staggering inversions of a life that contains not only new gifts but also harsh judgments against those who resist the vision or seek to have a piece of it on their own terms. The future held for us by the Bible is not a blissful blur. It is a promise of a historical future in which human dignity and human joy are valued and human worth is celebrated. This vision seriously challenges present arrangements for the sake of what is promised.

Moreover, this future, which staggers us by envisioning what we think not possible, offers the dynamic of a Promise-Maker and a Promise-Keeper—God. That is what is covenantal about this tradition. We are not in covenant with a good idea that is simply there or with our best intentions, which depend on us. We are in covenant with an active, caring, intervening God who keeps promises. Thus the Bible strangely affirms that we are to embrace the promise of a quite different society that *God* initiates. Yet this future to which we look forward is peculiarly historical, which is to say the future is breaking in now, and when it breaks in, it does so peculiarly among the powerless, despised, and weak. Bible reading is for the sake of remembering where we peculiarly come from and what is not peculiarly promised by this God who is graciously committed especially to those who have lost their utility and who have been written off by the world. The future here envisioned is not a withdrawal *from* history, but a renewal of humanness in history, so that the new humanness may emerge especially among those whom we treat with disdain. It is of course a shock and an affront to us to notice how the power of the Bible is especially received among the powerless. But we cannot avoid the evidence that it was especially the poor and powerless who responded to Jesus and who were able to trust God's promises. It may give us pause to wonder that the poor may be strangely open to such promises, and perhaps in our affluence, it becomes more difficult and problematic to let God's promises have power among us.

4. A covenantal-historical perspective *defines human existence in terms of vocation,* that is, not in the sense of an occupation but in terms of being called by our Covenant Partner to live in ways consistent with this relationship. We live not just because we happen to exist but because the One who has called the world into covenant is the same One who calls us to a relationship of responsibility. It is very difficult in our scientific world to understand this life-giving action of God. We are prone to think of creation as an act that simply lets people be. But creation is a call to be in a continuing relation with the caller. Existence therefore means to be continually answering the caller in new forms of fidelity and obedience. Our life is not for self-indulgence nor for desperate coping, nor for frantic, empty surviving. It is life lived after the manner of this very God who empties himself to obedience in the life of Jesus.

That is of course a more radical idea of God than we can readily entertain. In Jesus of Nazareth, we see not only a poor man, but we confess that in him we receive a whole new understanding of God. The Godness of God does not consist in his power and sovereignty but in his obedient suffering for the sake of the world. And we are bold to suggest that our vocation consists in that emptying activity after the manner of God. Clearly, such a radically different view of God requires of us a radically different view of ourselves. It suggests a whole new perception of what it means to be called to a vocation "in his image."

But it is not emptying as a simple spiritual discipline. It is rather emptying for the sake of healing, caring, and bringing newness. And this emptying action is not located simply in Jesus; it is the story of the whole of biblical history. Since God assumes vulnerability in caring for people, we are now called to make ourselves vulnerable in caring ways for our brothers and sisters. Out of this story, we realize that life is sterile and powerless when lived in isolation and aimlessness or even out of our fullness, but it is filled with the power to suffer in solidarity with the hurting ones so that they may be reconciled and rehabilitated. Vocation is then not simply what we do with our life, but it is in fact the very shape of our life. The call of God is to embrace the passion and suffering, to care for the weak, which God does all through biblical history.

The Biblical Invitation

Thus the Bible provides us with an alternative identity, an alternative way of understanding ourselves, an alternative way of relating to the world. It offers a radical and uncompromising challenge to our ordinary ways of self-understanding. It invites us to join in and to participate in the ongoing pilgrimage of those who live in the shattering of history, caring in ways that matter, secured by the covenanting God who is likewise on pilgrimage in history. This way of understanding our life lets us be open to hurts (crucifixions) but also to healing surprises of new life (resurrections) that emerge in our common life. The crucifixion of Jesus, like the pathos of God in the Hebrew Scriptures, provides a model for all the hurtful solidarity that may be practiced with the poor and the powerless. The resurrection of Jesus, like every life-giving act of God in the Hebrew Scriptures, provides a model for all the surprises of new life that happen among us, just when we think things are settled and closed. The surprises of the resurrection concern the emergence of expected new life in persons, in institutions, in social arrangements. And they come just when we think there are no more reasonable expectations.

Moreover, this way of understanding lets us embrace our own experience as important and the life of our brother and sister as part of our own. Most of all, it tells the story of this One who has committed his life to us, who promised in every hurting and rejoicing place in life to be there with us (Matt. 28:20). While other perspectives promise other things, this perspective finally promises that the Lord of glory, the One hidden and yet known, is there with us in all the hurting and healing of historical existence.

In our time, as perhaps in every time, the Bible provides standing ground against other attractive and seductive alternatives that we judge to be not so compelling for us.

1. Against a *modern-industrial-scientific* view of reality, the Bible asserts that we live in a world where healing mysteries surge among us. It is so hard for us to accept, but it is the case, from a biblical perspective, that God does do healing among the nations where no hope seemed likely. Persons do have their lives reoriented. Communities do express redeeming concern for the poor. Institutions do take actions toward justice. And such acts are often not logical or reasonable. But they do happen, just when the modern-industrial-scientific worldview thinks nothing more can happen. We are not called to be successful or secure but only faithful, to learn that in our risky caring, gifts of life are indeed given that sustain us.

2. Against *existentialism,* the Bible insists that life consists in communities of meaning. We not only invent meaning, but it comes to us from outside ourselves. Meanings are entrusted to us in the structures and institutions of common life but also in the flow of memory and vision between the generations.

3. Against *transcendentalism,* the Bible affirms that life's issues and ultimate meanings are situated precisely in the give-and-take of history. It denies that there is another realm of meaning to which we may appeal or withdraw.

This way of living lets us take God with real seriousness, to face God's sovereignty over us and freedom from us but also God's strange poverty among us that heals. It also lets us take ourselves and our lives seriously, knowing we are about something important. We can be serious about living but also buoyant because of our faithful Covenant Partner. Finally, this fresh perspective assures us, with all our mothers and fathers in faith before us, that we belong to our faithful God who is at work among us for our well-being, which is God's will for us.

All of this makes the Bible no easier to read. It is still strange because it does not accommodate our conventional language, images, or presuppositions. Rather, the Bible offers to us a way of perceiving reality that is very different from our usual forms of thought and speech. It requires of us a serious revamping of the way we think, speak, see, and live. It draws us into another history that is at odds with the public history commonly embraced by us. It also promises to us different gifts and demands. That fresh perspective concerns the church not just as a separate believing community but as a vision of a new humanity in his new creation. The Bible is keenly pertinent to our contemporary "crisis of the human spirit." The Bible provides hints of an alternative notion of what our humanness is, human in *history,* human in *covenant.*

For Reflection and Discussion

1. To what extent is covenant a way in which you might understand your life in relation to your church? in relation to your family?
2. What would it mean for you to think of God primarily as one who makes and keeps covenants?
3. What particular history shapes your life?
   - Who are the key actors?
   - What are the major events?
   - Does it contain surprises?
   - Does it include embarrassments?
   - Does it empower you? immobilize you?

Scripture Passages for Meditation

Gen. 9:8–17
Hos. 2:16–20
1 Cor. 11:23–26

Comment

The poem of Hos. 2:16–20 occurs in the history of Israel near the collapse of the Northern Kingdom when it fell to Assyria in 722. At that moment Israel felt deserted and was sure God had deserted her. Just then Hosea announces something startling about God: He makes covenant! He makes covenant with creation (v. 18). He disarms the enemy (v. 18). He takes a vow of fidelity that sounds like a marriage oath (vv. 19–20).

In 1 Cor. 11:23–26, Paul reports the church's confession that Eucharist is covenant-making. Each time the church eats at the Lord's table, it enters into a covenant of healing and discipline (v. 25). This covenant requires the biblical community of faith to enter a different history, to *remember* something special (v. 24) and to *expect* something special (v. 26).

God surprises the people by making a covenant when it seems least likely.

2

Nurturing
a Historical Imagination

The main theme of the Bible is covenantal history. It speaks of
a peculiar memory and promise, a very particular identity and
vocation. An important purpose of Bible reading and study is to
become a responsible participant in that covenantal history, to
share in its perceptions and nuances so that our life-world con-
forms to that which is central to the Bible. (By *life-world* I mean
the network of symbols, words, gestures, and images that give
meaning and coherence to our experience. The same experiences set in different life-worlds are experienced very differently. Thus a German and an Italian, to say nothing of a Tanzanian,
will experience the same event very differently. Here the case
is made that the life-world of the Bible is more sharply contrasted from all of these other life-worlds than they are from
each other.) But to be a responsible participant requires that we
read the Bible as insiders, and that is not easy. We are, on the
face of it, outsiders to its language and thought patterns, to its
cultural and historical assumptions. The following discussion
concerns the process by which we outsiders may read the Bible
as insiders, as participants in the covenantal history articulated
in the Bible.

Biblical faith is about joining another history. It is the story
of having memories other people cannot remember. It is the
story of having promises other people cannot envision. It is
about having an identity and vocation that others do not know
about or take seriously.

Because the Bible is so strange, all of us tend to be outsiders to its special life-world. Here we are concerned with the

process of nurture and discipline whereby outsiders to this life-world may enter into it. It is no easy matter to join into a different history and embrace its hopes, memories, and vocation. But that is the invitation of the Gospel of biblical faith. Now there is offered to us the possibility of participating in this different history.

If we are to share in, embrace, and take seriously this history that diverges sharply from our other one, many levels of relearning are necessary. The new learning includes entry into a new field of imagination. But there are also more mundane matters of chronology and geography that are essential to embracing this history. Some of this is not religiously rewarding but indispensable if we are to sense the particular nuance of the story.

In order to read the Bible intelligently, one needs the following:

1. a sense of its historical chronology, so that elements may be understood in proper relation to one another
2. an understanding of how each piece of literature is placed in that chronology
3. an appreciation of the geography of Canaan and the surrounding areas
4. an awareness of international relations, of how Israel interacted with the major peoples of the Fertile Crescent
5. a grasp of the major religio-cultural crises through which this people passed, for example, syncretism, urbanization, exile, establishment
6. a sense of the importance of major institutions in the life of the people, for example, monarchy, law, cultus

Obviously, all of these matters require close, careful, and extended study, and none of us can ever know as much of this as we might wish. We all operate with varying degrees of knowledge and ignorance. But such matters can be learned, and good books are available that serve as important beginning points.

The Need for Imagination

Such understanding of chronology and geography is indispensable for serious study of the Bible. But it will not make one an insider. I suggest that the key to becoming an insider (which presumes the above dimensions of knowledge) and therefore a participant in this covenantal-historical understanding of reality is the *nurturing of a historical imagination*. By *imagination* I mean an openness and sensitivity to the pulses of meaning that can be discerned in reflection upon historical experience preserved in a historical community. The imagination of the biblical community plays primarily with images that have come from this particular history. Thus Pharaoh comes to be a symbolic reference to every form of oppression. Bread comes to refer to the strange gift of nourishment that happens in the desert. And the stories cluster around these images, so that every oppression-liberation event is a new dealing with Pharaoh. Every surprising gift of nourishment is another miracle in the wilderness where starvation is wondrously avoided. This community, like every vital community, has its own energizing repertoire of images that give life and direction.

Such imagination of course opposes that kind of preoccupation with "facts" and "history" that believes only what can be proven and that limits belief to what is empirically demonstrable. Imagination is the gift of vitality that enables the believing community to discern possibility and promise, to receive newness and healing where others only measure and count and analyze. From generation to generation, the transmission of the Bible in all its power and vitality has been possible because people with imagination have been sensitive to fresh dimensions of meaning, to new interconnections perceived for the first time, to new glimpses of holiness that lie within the text. Conventionally, this openness to fresh nuances in the text has been located in the discussion of "inspiration and revelation," and I do not wish to deny those dimensions. But the need for imagination may also suggest that the handling of the text as an insider requires of us energy and boldness if its new pertinence is to be perceived and received among us.

Imagination Shaped by History

But the imagination of an insider is always an historical imagination. It is not just any innovative thinking; it is inventiveness driven and shaped by particular historical experiences. It is the capacity to return again and again to the concreteness of the past of this historical group—Israel or the church—and to discern there new meanings. The notions of *historical* (which means rooted to the meanings of a particular community) and *imagination* (which means open to surging pulses of meaning) are dialectical to each other. That is, the ideas of *historical* and *imagination* seem to move in opposite directions. Historical points back to precise, concrete, identifiable experiences. Imagination moves out into new and fresh symbolic overlays from the experience. Historical keeps the articulation concrete and particular, and imagination loses it in unexpected directions. But they are dialectical in that the two must be kept in tension, always correcting each other. Historical without imagination tends to be arid and not compelling. Imagination without historicality tends to turn to undisciplined fantasy. It is imagination that keeps the biblical past from being one-dimensional, dull, and closed, so that it is only a boring recital from long gone days. When handled with imagination, the tradition is seen to be a live memory always pressing into the present as a demand and a resource. It is a resource because the liberating energies given by God are found to be still given by God to the same confessing community. It is a demand because in that tradition we always discern in new ways the expectations of God to which we are called. Conversely, it is history that keeps imagination rooted and particular and under the discipline appropriate to this particular community. That discipline means that all imagination in the community of faith must be measured by the events and experiences remembered by us. The Exodus event, for example, requires that our perception be shaped by the gift of freedom and the protest against oppression, and this community is not free to think otherwise. Thus the imagination of Israel and the church is not any fanciful ruminating on any theme in any way; it is reflection on a defined stock of memories that shape and inform our present perception, attitudes, and behavior. Being an insider means nurturing a sense of the historical imagination of this community so that we begin to perceive and reflect and act as this community has always done.

Bread in the Wilderness

Here we shall consider one such dimension of historical imagination as an illustration of how such a practice might help us understand the Bible and let us be insiders to its faith and power. While we will focus on one dimension, a variety of others might equally well be chosen. Exodus 16 is the story of Israel being led and fed in the wilderness. It is a story that is very old and long treasured by Israel. And we may believe it was an important one in Israel's historical imagination, that is, in her inventive meditation on her particular past. It is clear that the process of the Bible itself is a process of historical imagining exercised on stories like this one, so that fresh nuances are continually discerned in the old story. The narrative of Exodus 16 concerns this people having left the slavery of Egypt on the way to a land of promise. But between departure from slavery and the entry to secure, good land, there is this long, demanding wilderness stay.

Wilderness, a central Biblical image, is a place of precariousness without food, without defense or resource. The center of this memory is in the wonder that in this place where death seemed certain, God is present, having also submitted to the conditions of the desert. God is there with surprising, unexpected, and unexplained food. The Bible does not try to explain but only articulates amazement. Out of that event, Israel formed a central focus of historical imagination: the bread of the wilderness is the bread of heaven!

That bread is contrasted with the bread of slavery, which is safe but gives neither life nor freedom. That bread is contrasted with the bread of the promised land, which will be good but which we do not yet possess. That bread is contrasted with the starvation of the desert, for Israel feared death and yet lived! Out of that event, Israel learned something crucial about the Lord God, that God is a very present help in time of trouble (cf. Ps. 46:1) in order to do the strange life-giving thing when it seems impossible. Israel learned about the wilderness of life, that though it seems forlorn and hopeless, it is a place of nourishment because the Lord is there. Israel learned something about its life, that Israel is to live in fragile dependence, not by submitting to secure slaveries nor by owning predictable bakeries, but by being present to the Lord even in the wilderness and living by God's remarkable bread.

That event has become a prism through which Israel and the church understand life. It is not the only such prism, but it is a central one among the several offered in the Bible. The gift of manna is such an elemental event because all of us hunger and yearn to be filled: all of us crave nourishment and sometimes receive and sometimes do not. All of us have a chance to give food to others or withhold it. And each time Israel and the church faced the event of feeding or being fed, this elemental story was turned to be seen in yet another way. Israel and the church have been enormously inventive in handling this memory, but the community is disciplined and limited by the original prism: that in a place of death, life was given amazingly by the Lord. This story with always new nuances is told from generation to generation among the faithful. We live as insiders in a history in which feeding and being fed is a sign and a focus for faith. Outside of this historical imagination, such acts might be experienced but not loaded with these particular meanings. But insiders discern in such moments that which is denied to and hidden from outsiders.

Some Biblical Uses of This Story

Among the uses made of this story in the subsequent retellings are at least the following. In Isa. 55:1–3, a poem for exiles when the community of Israel in the sixth century B.C.E. is hopeless, starved for faith as well as for bread, it is asserted that bread is freshly given and milk is for the taking. This poet, one of our comrades in faith, has taken the manna story and has presented it in yet another form so that his contemporaries can see their situation differently. Exile, like the wilderness sojourn, seems hopeless and without signs of life. But for people who remember imaginatively, exile, like wilderness, is seen to be a place where God freely nourishes his desperate people. Deathly places, wilderness, or exile are, because of Yahweh, places of life. In this poetry of Isaiah 55, it is not self-evident that the poet consciously alludes to Exodus 16, and perhaps he does not. But the theme floats in the life of this people, and listeners to such poetry make connections out of their stock of historical memory. And quite clearly, whether intended by the poet or not, the link between the old narrative and the new poetry enlivens both. Both take on fresh meanings that yield power and insight for a community in a seemingly hopeless situation.

In the Christian Testament, the Gospel of Mark records two feeding actions of Jesus. In 6:30–44 he feeds five thousand and in 8:1–10 he feeds four thousand. Obviously the actions of Jesus are understood quite differently because the remembering church saw his actions through the prism of the manna story, and no doubt Jesus himself also did. It is clearly intended to suggest that this old history of life-giving food in a place of death is happening again. The narrative in Mark is quite self-consciously inventive in the use of history. It is imaginative in its presentation, but its imagination is rooted in a precise historical memory. As a result, Jesus is presented not simply as a miracle-worker or a breadmaker but as the action of God transforming a "wilderness" (cf. Mark 6:35; 8:4) into a place of nourishment, a place of abandonment into one of caring power, a place of death into a time of life. Jesus, as the power of God, transforms the situation. And as the church remembered and told this story and reflected on it, it drew a powerful conclusion: We are in covenant with the transforming one. It has been so since our fathers and mothers in Exodus 16, and it is so each time we eat in the presence of this holy power.

It will be clear to you that in reporting this story I have handled it like an insider. By "insider" I do not mean one who has special expertise or technical learning. Rather I mean one who lives in and derives life from the community that believes these materials. Insiders are all the people who believe that these memories tell us about *our* past and these promises tell us about *our* future. Outsiders, by contrast, do not take the

materials that seriously but regard them only as interesting materials that we can take or leave as they suit us. Only an insider
would make the connections to Exodus 16 in a way that ener-
gizes and informs the Mark narrative. This connection has been
made by the narrators of Mark who are also insiders, but they
do it so subtly that it takes insiders to recognize the sensitivity
and suggestion of the way the story is told. We are engaged in
serious Bible study when we are alert and responsive to such
interactions among the texts.

In Mark 8:14–21, Jesus and the earliest church (the disciples) reflect on the meaning of the bread. The narrative makes
clear on the one hand that they know there is an overplus of
meaning here, the overplus of God in history among his people
in the person of Jesus. On the other hand, it is clear that they
do not really grasp the power of the image nor the reality presented in the miracle of nourishment because it calls into question every presupposition and self-interest they have. Thus our
hardness of heart (cf. 6:52) sometimes blocks us from full appreciation of our historical imagination. Indeed, becoming insiders to this covenantal historical perspective requires that we
face up to our hardness of heart and receive the gift of a new
heart. In other words, serious Bible study done by insiders expects these texts will affect our life so that we see things differently and are required to make fresh decisions about our values
and priorities, about our fears and hopes. Hard-heartedness is
evidenced both in Pharaoh and in the opponents of Jesus who
resist the newness of God and want to keep things the way
they are. But reading these stories with a new heart means that
fresh decisions are made about our identity and the ways in
which we face the questions of freedom, order, and justice.

In John 6, in a more difficult and sophisticated discussion,
the Exodus 16 story is again recalled so that Jesus may be understood. In Mark 6:8, the manna story is only alluded to in order to illuminate Jesus, who seems to fulfill that story. But here
in John 6, the event of Jesus and of the manna are contrasted
so that Jesus and not manna is the true bread of God. Whereas
Mark had maintained continuity between old story and new
event, the Fourth Gospel proceeds by way of contrast. On the
other hand, it is clear that Jesus cannot be understood apart

from the old memory. Jesus is here presented as the unexpected gift of God that transforms situations from hunger to fullness, from death to life. It is not too much to hint that feeding someone who is desperately hungry causes them to be "revived," that is, caused to live again. Thus the feeding is a resurrection event, and we may discern in each of these narratives a bold perception of the gospel of resurrection.

The stories in Mark present Jesus as the one who offers bread. The bread he offers is surely the gospel that makes things new. But the argument is shifted in the story in John so that Jesus himself is now the bread of life. Eating this bread means accepting his rule and claim over us and becoming one with his body. Eating the bread, that is, embracing Jesus, leads to new joys and satisfactions that cannot be had from another bread, that is, any other gospel. Thus the story shifts from Mark to John. And in extending the meaning of the feeding narrative, it is not a far step to understand that in preserving these stories, the early church was also alluding to the Eucharist as the form in which the church still feasts on the bread of life.

The giving and receiving of the bread that is the body is the self-giving of God in a way that transforms situations. In the feeding process, now experienced as the Eucharist, it is not only the bread that is changed in character by sacramental action. It is also the believing community that is changed. The church receives the bread, in the old story of manna or in the present practice of Eucharist, always in the face of death and is surprised by life. That feeding calls the believing community away from the deathly promises and perceptions of the culture around us. That culture around us eats other bread and makes other promises, but it cannot give life. It is only the bread that this community has always hoped for that will give life. No wonder that the early church knew him in the "breaking of bread" (Luke 24:35). Such narratives do not yield a full theology of Eucharist, for that is not the function of historical imagination. They do permit us, however, to discern our life differently because of the root memories that inform us.

The miracle of feeding is not only a present gift in the Eucharist. The bread received in the feeding sacrament is of course a present reality. It is given here and now and it makes a difference. But it is also an expectant eating, which is done "until he comes." There is a waiting by the hungry for the full action of God. As Mary affirmed, "He has filled the hungry with good things, / and sent the rich away empty" (Luke 1:53). The miracle of feeding is also a demand (*a*) to face daily the dependence of our life upon this amazing one (Matt. 6:11), (*b*) to give bread as God has done, precisely to those who cannot claim it (Luke 14:12–14), and (*c*) to know that the future of our life is ultimately shaped by the way in which we share the miracle of bread entrusted to us (Matt. 25:35).

The imagery of the manna story is used by Paul even in the handling of a church dispute about how people relate to each other in the believing community in time of need. In the context of the manna story that he quotes (2 Cor. 8:15), Paul makes this remarkable statement about Jesus: "Though he was rich, yet for your sakes he became poor, so that by his poverty you might become rich" (2 Cor. 8:9). This experience of the bread is offered as a model for the church in dealing with problems and resources in a way that is consistent with its historical imagination. Clearly Paul discerns how radical is the power of the text.

Some Lines of Reflection on the Story

Such a symbol as giving bread unexpectedly to people starving in the wilderness is a fluid, open symbol that can be turned in many ways and used in many different contexts. I can think of at least four major lines of reflection that grow out of this narrative and this theme that insiders can pursue:

1. Fresh understandings of Eucharist as the miracle of nourishment for us who are always in the context of death.
2. New reflections on our concern for world hunger, to reflect on the gift of resources we only know to be available when we take risks in places of death.
3. The new bread offers a sharp criticism of our entire consumer society and its values where we eat and eat and are never satisfied because we have substituted our bread for the bread of life. Now there is another bread that can never

be managed by us, but it leaves us satisfied and able to expose the false bread offered us.

4. The new reception of bread from such a gracious source permits a *rejection of the kind of technical reason* that knows so much and explains everything, but is helpless in the face of unexpected life-giving gifts. It is still the case that our hard heart prevents us from understanding the bread!

Obviously there are many other dimensions to the theme that will be suggested to us as we engage in historical imagination. Such a text can serve to dramatically reshape so many of our perceptions, can invite us to new resources and awarenesses, can critique the controlling values of our culture, and can permit us to embrace new directions for our life.

This text and motif, like other central memories, present the richness of the Gospel, the power of our tradition, and the possibility of another stance in life. Building upon the study of literature, history, geography, and such like, this practice of historical imagination is open only to insiders who participate in the history of this people. To others, these narratives seem like isolated and archaic stories to be easily passed over. But to insiders they are to be cherished and treasured and explored for pluses of meaning we value for coming generations.

A study of such symbols, firmly rooted in history but inviting full play of imagination, is not easy because it is fluid and unsure, and there are no single right answers. It is that which keeps Scripture study always interesting and rewarding. And it is for that reason that we cannot settle for a single translation of the Bible. Each translation is an attempt to discern some of the richness in the symbolism entrusted to this historical community. Such exploration requires the energy of the entire community of insiders and not only academic or ecclesiastical experts, for any one brother or sister might catch a nuance all the others have missed. Scripture study, among other things, is like a feast. Sometimes even the text can be transforming bread of life. The text does feed people toward newness. Undoubtedly the energy of the civil rights movement in our country was generated by this historical imagination. New possibilities and fresh courage for facing the crisis of poverty are being derived from these texts. And in countless unknown and unnamed places, the people of God are finding new ways of living and risking in mission because these memories have presented new possible futures and new present vocations. Because it is miraculously given, we can feed each other—new life might come!

For Reflection and Discussion

1. To have "imagination" means to be open to the notion that experiences and words and symbols have many meanings and not only one:
    *   Tell about an imaginative person who has made a difference in your life.
    *   Tell about a person in your life who has no imagination, that is, who thinks everything has one meaning.
    *   Think of situations in which you have been an imaginative person.
2. "Bread" is a rich symbol for our living:
    *   Tell about a time when you have been especially hungry and then fed.
    *   Recall the happiest meal in your life.
    *   Can you think of a time when you ate too much? Why did it happen? Are these satisfactions which do not give joy, power, or new life?
3. Think of four possible imaginative meanings for eucharistic bread.

Scripture Passages for Meditation

Isa. 5:1–7
Hos. 9:10
Matt. 21:33–46
John 15:1–11

Comment

We have reviewed several texts with the theme of bread. Above are some texts with the theme of vine. In many poetic passages the vine is Israel, the people of God. God himself is the vine keeper. God cares for Israel. The vine keeper cares for the vine.

The vine is expected to produce grapes. In the eighth century B.C.E., the prophets spoke of Israel as a vine that never produced any good grapes.

The same image is used in the Christian Scriptures for the church. The vine keeper still protects the vine and expects grapes from the vine. Can you think of good grapes from the vine? How about sour grapes?

3

Making Sense
as an Insider

The Bible is a strange book that is put together in an odd way. It seems to have no order at all but is a jumbled collection hard to penetrate. It will not do to read it from cover to cover as faithful believers have often done, and it is not much better to try to read it chronologically (even if we could date all of the materials, which we cannot). It is not helpful to try to impose on the literature an order that reflects modern scientific under- standings. As much as we are able, we can try to read the Bible like insiders and let the material itself determine the order for us. Of course that is not completely possible, but if we take se- riously the *shape of tradition,* we may discover clues that will let us see the material from the inside. In what follows, I shall try to be sensitive to the *function of the literature.* It is likely the case that if we can determine the function of the literature, we shall understand how it stands in relation to the other parts of the collection.

The Primal Narrative

I suggest that the place to begin in determining the shape of the tradition is with the *primal narrative,* that most simple, ele- mental, and nonnegotiable story line that lies at the heart of biblical faith. Such a narrative is presented with the passion of fresh believers and with the simplicity of a community that had screened out all uncertainties and felt no reason to explain. It is an affirmation in story form that asserts, "This is the most important story we know, and we have come to believe it is decisively about us." This story is clearly for the insiders, and no effort at all is made to persuade or convince outsiders.

Gerhard von Rad, noted German scholar, has suggested that Israel's primal narrative (his word is *credo*)—the consistently believed in and recited root story that a community relies upon in crisis and the one by which the truth or falseness of every other story is judged—can be located in three texts:

1. Deut. 26:5–9, a liturgical confession that Israel recites as the offering is brought before the altar. The offering is a crucial statement of loyalty and allegiance, and in that context Israel asserts her deepest and most precious story.
2. Deut. 6:20–24, a teaching recital in response to the stylized question of a child. It has been suggested that this is a formula for catechetical instruction, though it is the child who asks and the parents who answer (not a bad catechetical method).
3. Josh. 24:1–13, a speech before a national assembly in which Israel is constituted as a self-conscious covenantal community, some think for the first time. The assembly consists of all kinds of people with diverse stories. Here is declared to them the one story that is now to be the shared ground for their common life.

Since Von Rad, other scholars have suggested that Exod. 15:1–18 may be a much earlier and more convincing example of the primal narrative than those cited by Von Rad. It is likely that Exodus 15 is the earliest presentation we have of such a normative statement of faith, but that difference from Von Rad is not important for the point being made here. It is a recital just after the deliverance from slavery in which Israel asserted her deepest confession in an exalted mood of jubilation.

Von Rad has made it clear that these assertions come behind and before any reasoned theology or any apologetic concern to justify faith to outsiders. They are the assertions that Israel knew intuitively to be true and that she eagerly asserted in situations of urgency when it was necessary to announce her peculiar historical identity.

In a similar way, C. H. Dodd, noted English scholar, has observed that in the Christian Testament, we may discern a primal narrative that brings to us the basic substance of the earliest preaching (his word is *kerygma*) of the church and therefore the earliest faith of the church. It seems most likely that the earliest statements of such faith do not come from the Gospel accounts but from statements in the letters of Paul. Paul apparently relied on the oral traditions of the early church, the same oral traditions that were used for the forming of the Gospels. Thus the statements in the letters to Corinth are likely earlier than the Gospel accounts, though they surely report the same faith:

1. In 1 Cor. 1:23, the primal narrative is articulated as the substance of preaching.
2. In 1 Cor. 3:1, it is presented as the foundation of all Christian faith, which means it is the most elemental statement of faith that can be made. As for all narratives of this kind, there are no theological presuppositions or assertions behind them. This is the bedrock of the faith of the church.
3. In 1 Cor. 15:3–8, it is presented as the essential tradition that is remembered by the church in its theological reflection.

Now the *credo* of Israel discerned by Von Rad and the *kerygma* of the church articulated by Dodd are quite different from each other for obvious reasons. The one is formulated by a community concerned with Israel's faith, and the other by a community focused on the events of Jesus' presence and ministry. The one is cast in completely Semitic idiom, and the other is presented in a Hellenistic context. The one is the product of long and not very well understood processes; whereas the other appeared in a relatively short time. But they have important similarities that are decisive for understanding the real intent of the biblical tradition:

a. Both are recitals of *acts of God* that have radically changed life for those who affirm them. The decisive grammar of biblical faith presents an active verb with God himself as the subject and the church or the world as the object of the verb, that is, as the recipient of God's action.

b. Both are statements of confession or assertion that make no attempt to explain or prove. They are bold, primitive affirmations of faith, stripped of every ornamentation or justification.

c. Both are narratives that recite ways in which God has acted to change the shape of the entire historical process. That is, they tell of God introducing the cause of freedom in a society that was characteristically oppressive. They tell of the capacity for life to be wrought out of situations of hopelessness and death. And since these events have happened, human consciousness cannot be the same. It is now known by those who have faced this evidence that real newness can come into human history that is not derived from old forms and patterns. Concrete events like the healing of a man or the finding of a baby have now been given universal significance. The finding of the baby is an announcement to the arrangers of this world that a new world is promised by God and will come. The healing of a man is understood as a dismantling of the old arrangements that kept people from being human. The impact of these memories concerns both the shape of public life and the images we have of our personal existence. The substance of these kernels of biblical faith (*credo, kerygma*) presents the essentials of all of biblical faith. For Israel:

1. A *promise* was made to our forebears in the midst of great precariousness.
2. God *delivered* Israel from slavery to freedom with a great show of power that defeated the greatest power of the time.
3. God led Israel *in the wilderness,* a place of precarious pilgrimage, and nourished and sustained the people.
4. God brought Israel to the *good land* that God had promised.

For the early church, as Dodd has summarized:
1. The prophecies are fulfilled, and the *New Age* is inaugurated by the coming of Christ.
2. He was born of the *seed of David.*
3. He *died* according to the Scriptures, to deliver us out of the present evil age.
4. He was *buried.*
5. He *rose* on the third day according to the Scriptures.
6. He is *exalted* at the right hand of God, as son of God and Lord of the living and dead.
7. He *will come again* as Judge and Savior of humankind.

To this summary might be added, although Dodd did not do so, the outpouring of the Spirit as the effect of Jesus' exaltation.

These two lists provide a summary of biblical faith in broad outline and may provide us with a way of understanding the strange ordering of the literature.

The Expanded Narrative

After understanding the primal narrative, we may next speak of the *expanded narrative*. Obviously the biblical text now presents to us all kinds of materials that do not have the clarity or conciseness of the credo or kerygma. In the process of building the tradition, the primal narrative was expanded over a period of time in ways that seem to us not very careful or disciplined. Rather, they give the impression of being careless and disordered. The primal narratives have attracted to them all kinds of diverse material that may or may not be related to the themes of the primal narrative. But they have been pressed into relationship with the primal themes and into their service. That is, they have been brought into contact with this central story and have had their meanings changed by it. In reading this more extended material, it is helpful in each case to consider it as a more elaborate and complete presentation of the same theme found in the kernel, which means that this literature also is confessional and not reportorial in character.

Thus in Genesis, chapters 12—50, the story of Abraham, Isaac, Jacob, and Joseph is an extended presentation of the promise made to "my father who is a wandering Aramean." And in each unit of Genesis 12—50, we may look for the promise being kept to the precarious ("wandering") one. For those who read as insiders, the central issue of these texts is whether God will keep the promise. The stories in their present form reflect doubt and uncertainty. They also reflect calculation and manipulation by persons who could not rest on the promises but had a better way of their own. Often the stories agonize because God does not seem ready or able to keep the promise of giving a son; the next generation then must also bear the promise. Can the barren woman become the mother of the child of promise (Genesis 18:1–15)? Can the younger son secure the promise that should have gone elsewhere (Genesis 27)? Can the beloved son come out of the pit to power (Genesis 40—41)? These are all dimensions of the single statement of the old credo.

As Israel told the story with imaginative attentiveness to detail, the primal narrative became handled and illuminated in many ways over a long period of time in many different circumstances. In the same way, for the early church, it seems probable that different communities in different places told the stories in different ways. The communities related to Matthew, and Luke knew and valued the birth stories as the community of Mark did not. Each community arranged the materials differently to serve its own purposes and each had different memories about Easter.

The expanded narrative is a collection of all the ways in which the primal narrative has been perceived and handled. So with the other themes in the credo of Israel:

The assertion of deliverance from Egypt (Deut. 6:21–22; 26:6–8; Josh. 24:5–7) is expanded into the fulsome story of Exodus 1—15.

The memory of wilderness sojourn is now extended into Exodus 16—18 and Numbers 10—24.

The affirmation of the gift of the land is elaborated in Joshua 1—12.

The brief confessional statement has become a longer statement with many curious components, each of which asserts Israel's basic faith. Some scholars have called the extended form an *epic* derived from the *credo.*

In the Christian Testament, the primal narrative has been extended to become the whole Gospel narrative of the birth, life, ministry, death, resurrection, and ascension of Jesus. The primal narrative focuses rather exclusively on the last events and the fuller Gospel narrative is filled out with memories of his life and ministry. But even that is not mere biography. It consists rather of memories seen through the prism of the dominant theme of crucifixion and resurrection, so that many stories in the Gospels are episodes where, by Jesus' presence, action, and words, a deathly situation was turned to life (cf. Mark

5:24–34; Luke 7:36–50; Luke 19:1–10). Thus for an insider, even these narratives, seemingly removed from the primal narrative, do present that same faith. The narratives of the Hexateuch (Genesis to Joshua) and the Gospels embody many attempts by many persons and groups over a long period of time to define the basic credo-kerygma, given their particular understandings.

Derivative Narratives

In both the Hebrew Scriptures and the Christian Testament, this literature had peculiar primacy. But each community had a subsequent history told in what we may call *derivative narrative* that is, the history of (*a*) Israel after Moses-Joshua and (*b*) the church after Jesus. In both cases, the community of faith could not keep retelling the old story. As time passed, new experiences happened that were incorporated into the story. Thus the *old primal story* was supplemented by an *ongoing tradition.* Though this also belongs to the self-identifying process of the community, in neither case is this derivative material regarded with the same seriousness or authority. In the Hebrew Scriptures, this derivative narrative, which includes all the books from Judges through Nehemiah, reports the life, faith, and actions of the believing community as it worked its difficult way through changing historical circumstances with varying degrees of faithfulness and fickleness. In the Christian Testament, this derivative literature is the Book of Acts, which presents the actions of the Apostles through several crises in the early church. In neither case is this pure reporting of a historical chronicle. In both cases, it is a theological statement about how the spirit of God has ruled the history of this people, the bearers of a new presence in history.

Thus much of Israel's derivative narrative concerns the power of God's word to work its will, that is, to keep the promises announced earlier (cf. 1 Kings 8:20; 12:15; 15:29; 16:12,34; 21:27–29; 22:35; 2 Kings 1:17; 23:16–18; 23:30; 24:2). Similarly in the Christian Testament, the story ostensibly reports the actions of leaders in the church, but it is also the history of God's spirit (Acts 2:17–18; 6:10; 18:5; 19:21) or of God's word (Acts 6:7; 8:4; 12:24; 19:20) at work in a new way in history. Presumably the narrative could have been presented as "objective reporting." But for an insider it is important to recognize the intensely believing character of the material. To fail to see this is to miss the point of the literature. In each case, this narrative takes the primal memory of the basic narrative and testifies to its power and authority in the life of the ongoing community that is removed in time from the primal events but still is powered by their enduring impact. Clearly, in both cases, this can only in a very special way be called "history" because it is history in which the Lord of the primal narrative plays the central and crucial role. Only insiders can understand what that means for our history as well as for our sacred literature.

The Literature of Institutionalization

Of course every enduring community, including those formed in the zeal of a fresh religious commitment, must organize its life to preserve its initial intent; to guard against perversion; to define the structure of order, the role of leadership, and the scope of freedom; and to deal with specific internal problems and concerns. The literature reporting these facets of the history of the community we may call the *literature of institutionalization,* which is often several generations removed from the original leadership, for only then do such problems surface with their full import and danger.

This literature, crucial for the community itself, often does not make for exciting reading. In the Hebrew Scriptures, it includes the dreary texts of Exodus 25—40, the Book of Leviticus, Numbers 1—10 and 25—36, and in a removed way, Ezekiel 40—48. This literature is designed to authorize and legitimate forms of leadership, customs and mores, as well as liturgical practice. In the Christian Testament, in quite another genre (presented as letters), we may identify 1 and 2 Timothy and Titus as literature of institutionalization, showing the faithful community dealing with the daily tasks of order, survival, maintenance, and discipline.

The Literature of Mature Theological Reflection

Much more interesting and edifying is another kind of literature we may designate as the *literature of mature theological reflection*. Nothing in the Bible comes close to sustained, systematic thought that is self-conscious about epistemology or method. Thus all of it stays primitive in its idiom and boldly free in its confessional character. But we may observe that Deuteronomy and Romans respectively seem to some authorities to be the most eloquent and ripest insights of the reflective community of faith.

In Deuteronomy, the central issues concern the power of covenant and the rule of covenantal law in a community tempted to syncretism. Deuteronomy is a literature that concerns the community of faith when it is seriously compromised with other religious values and perceptions. Perhaps this temptation is the fertility religion of Canaan. Or perhaps it is the oppressive imperial religion of Assyria. Either way, the Israelites apparently found it attractive to incorporate foreign influences into their religion in ways that seriously perverted the meaning of covenant with the God of Israel. Deuteronomy is written in protest against such syncretism and in order to reassert the faith of Israel in its less contaminated form. In Romans (again in the form of a letter), the reflective issue concerns the meaning and significance of a religion of grace. These two books lie at the confessional, theological center of the Bible and seek to say most forcefully what the primal narrative had asserted. They are both attempts to take up the claim of the primal narrative and give it more cohesive and comprehensive expression.

The Literature of Instruction and Vocation

Finally we may identify the *literature of instruction and vocation* that includes the prophetic (Isaiah to Malachi) and sapiential (Job to Ecclesiastes) literature of the Hebrew Scriptures and the Epistles (1 Corinthians to Jude) of the Christian Testament. These are texts in which the preacher-teachers of the community have announced the claims of faith in a particular situation.

This literature is quite diverse, and this category is rather a catchall in which a function justifies the grouping, namely, the attempt to say what this faith means in a particular situation. This literature includes wisdom sayings as in Proverbs and James that seem quite removed from the primal narrative, as well as the agonies of the poetry of Job and the sophisticated theological ruminations of Hebrews. At times this literature is essentially *instructional* in character. This is true not only of the wisdom pieces we have mentioned. It is also true of Paul's letters, which often contain instructional material about how the church is to deal with specific situations. At other times, these are essentially *lyrical* in character as in the Psalms and some of the hymnic fragments in the Letters (as in Phil. 2:5–11 and Col. 1:15–20). In this grouping, I would also include *visionary* materials commonly labeled "apocalyptic" (Daniel, Revelation), which are attempts by a weary and desperate community to articulate a form of rationality that would maintain freedom for faith in an oppressive context. But functionally this literature is the same, for it seeks to assert the primal narrative in a way of power and authority for a special circumstance. Out of all these times and in these various ways (instructional, lyrical, visionary), these materials are presented with the passion of those who consider this faith the only option.

This singular passion is most evident in the prophets of Israel, whom I have included in the literature of instruction and vocation. It is the prophets who insist that the primal narrative has power, authority, and relevance in all kinds of new situations. Indeed, a proper understanding of the prophets, as of the Epistles, requires linking them to the primal narrative.

The Relationship of These Kinds of Literature

The categories suggested here should not be pressed, for they are only an introductory scheme for orientation and will not hold up under detailed scrutiny. But they are enough to note how all of the literature can be understood by insiders as the way our community has faced the question of identity and mission.

Finally we may make some suggestions about the intricate relationship that these various literatures have to one another.

I have urged that all parts are related to and informed by the primal narrative. Everything must be assessed by those assertions. The next most important assertions are the expanded narratives that mean to deal with the same claims and substance as the primal narrative. We are more removed in the derivative narrative, for it features the confessing community as it becomes more removed in time from the primal events. However, even this material seeks to show the claims of the primal narrative in the continuing community that recites them. The last three groupings, the literature of institutionalization, the literature of mature theological reflection, and the literature of instruction and vocation, are all functions of the derivative literature. That is, they deal with three tasks that the community must address if it is to be faithful to the primal narrative: it must (*a*) organize its life, (*b*) articulate its best understandings, and (*c*) locate specific contacts between faith and life. Such an understanding organizes the material in this way:

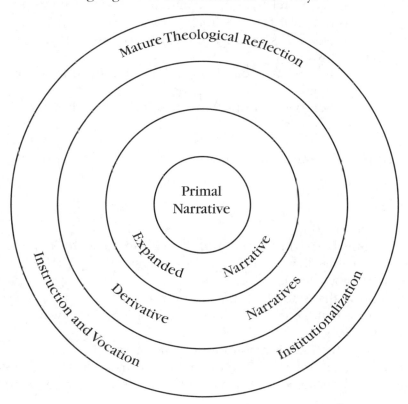

As strange as it all seems, insiders know that our mothers and fathers in faith for many generations have sought to understand and live all of life in response to the covenanting God who brings slaves out of bondage and who brings life out of death. That focus sets all the literature in context.

For Reflection and Discussion

1. What is the "basic story" of your life? Name the two or three or four basic events or perceptions that shape your life.
   - Which parts of that are "good news"?
   - Which parts are "bad news"?
2. Israel's credo is about going out from a place (Jer. 2:6) and coming in to a new place (Jer. 2:7).
   - In your basic story, what safe places, safe relationships, safe connections have you been able to risk in pilgrimage? Has this permitted you to grow?
   - What places, relationships, connections have been too precious to leave? Has this immobilized or protected you?
3. The Christian Testament church first confessed that Jesus died and was raised.
   - In your life, have you died to what is old in your person? What would you like to die to?
   - Have you been surprised by new life? Where in your life might it come?

Scripture Passages for Meditation

Mark 10:17–22
Acts 3:1–10

Comment

In his book *A Place for You,* Paul Tournier writes that the task of mature living consists in two things:
1. finding a safe place for yourself
2. leaving that safe place in a new venture

Of course that means one is never safe for long but always between places.

Mark 10:17–22 is not just a story about one rich man; it is a model for discipleship. The one whom Jesus addresses (that's us) is called to *give* away what he has and *come* with Jesus, to leave his place and go in venture to a new place of faith. And that one cannot because the place of his riches is too safe. The Gospel of Mark is probably out of the early congregation in Rome, which had each day to decide between faith in Jesus and the demands of the emperor. Some days it is hard to choose the venture of faith against the safety of establishment reality.

The narrative of these texts concerns the amazing power of the Christ. Because the disciples had themselves left things to go on pilgrimage with Jesus, they had the power to move other people from a place of hopelessness (Acts 3:2) to new life (v. 7). They did a resurrection act. They addressed a man who belonged nowhere and gave him a safe place in the Gospel.

The church and its members are still promised power to move people, but it depends on a decision to leave our own safe place as Israel has always been called to do.

The call of the Gospel is to leave what is organized against the promises of God and to be on the way to the place where God's purposes have power. It is a call that takes the form of demand because such leaving is abrasive and painful. It is a call that takes the form of a gift, because the place of promise is never invented by us. It is always given by God in ways we cannot imagine or control.

4

The Center
of the Odd Perspective
of the Bible—God

Many peculiar characteristics of the Bible do not fit into our conventional notions about religion. Sometimes these peculiar features are an embarrassment to us, but they are also precious to us. The most important peculiarity—hardest to understand, most precious to us—is not about literature or culture or history. It is not about the strange customs of people or the strange turns of political history. Rather it is about God.

The God of the Bible is the strangest thing about the whole Bible. In all the history of religion, there is no other like the God of the Bible. And that is hard to understand. So the peoples who dealt with God in the Bible always wanted to relate to the Divine Self like they related to all other notions of God. And in every time, even ours, we are tempted to force God into other categories as though God belongs to a species of similar agents.

But God is not like any other. And God's strangeness is in this. God is *with people*. God is *for people*. God's goodness is not in the great transcendental power nor in the majestic remoteness nor in the demanding toughness but in the readiness to be with and for people. And this being with and for is not a matter of bribery or deception or intimidation. God simply wills it so. God is not, in a characteristic way, *by God's self,* but *for others*.

As suggested earlier, a central theme of the Bible is *covenant,* the notion of making commitments and keeping them, of making promises and fulfilling them. This theme emerges as central in the Bible because God's self-revelation showed a covenant-making, covenant-keeping God.* That is who God is. That is how the Divine Self meets Israel and relates to the church. That is how God relates to creation as a faithful covenant-keeper. That is how God defines our world for us as a process of covenant-making and covenant-keeping. And that is the good news of the Gospel, that God is faithful to the Covenant.

In the Hebrew Scriptures, we may observe four dimensions of God as the covenant-maker who gives people the strength and joy of life in covenant.

Now You Are God's People

The Exodus, the focal event of Israel's faith, is the announcement that the Lord is actively engaged for the people. In answer to their cries for help, God asserts: "I have observed the misery of my people. . . . I have heard their cry. . . . I know their sufferings, and I have come down to deliver them" (Exod. 3:7–8). That is who God is. This is where biblical faith begins. The fourfold statement builds. The first two suggest only that God observes the trouble. The third affirms that God takes it seriously. But the fourth is decisive. God is actively engaged for the slaves, coming into the crisis on behalf of the helpless ones. This powerful intervention for Israel is not for the sake of anybody honorable or worthy or impressive (Deut. 7:6–8; 9:6); it is an ignoble lot ("rabble," Exod. 12:38; Num. 11:4) to whom God makes this commitment. The Lord's covenant-making activity not only adds to the well-being of the people, enhancing what already existed. It also creates a people who did not exist and gives them well-being when they had none:

---

*In the Hebrew Scriptures, the name by which God described himself to Moses on Mount Sinai is written YHWH. The *Jerome Biblical Commentary* sums up a long discussion on the meaning and use of this name by saying that it is "the Israelite name for God by which the association of Yahweh and Israel is mutually accepted and proclaimed" (p. 738). The more than twenty-five-hundred-year-old reverential custom of substituting the word *Lord* for the sacred name *YHWH* is followed in this book.

Once you were not a people,
>   but now you are God's people;
once you had not received mercy,
>   but now you have received mercy.

(1 Pet. 2:10)

God's faithful being with and being for calls Israel into existence when it did not exist (Rom. 4:17). It is no wonder that at the end of the Exodus story in the great celebrative poem, Israel asserts the rhetorical question:

"Who is like you, O LORD, among the gods?
>   Who is like you, majestic in holiness,
>   awesome in splendor, doing wonders?

(Exod. 15:11)

And the obvious answer is: nobody. God's majesty involves a surprising commitment to the nobodies. Thus God is praised as the supreme God: "For the LORD your God is God of gods and Lord of lords, the great God, mighty and awesome" (v. 17). But the doxology continues: "[God] executes justice for the orphan and the widow, and . . . loves the strangers, providing them food and clothing" (Deut. 10:18).

God Present with Power

This Lord is an active agent who *comes and is present with power*. God is not inclined toward the people by positive sentiment or a kindly feeling. The Lord acts powerfully on behalf of Israel when Israel is helpless and has no power of its own. Thus in the Exodus story, these assertions are made:

"The LORD will fight for you, and you have only to keep
>   still." (14:14)
"Let us flee from the Israelites, for the LORD is fighting for
>   them against Egypt." (V. 25)
The LORD tossed the Egyptians into the sea. (V. 27)
Thus the LORD saved Israel that day from the Egyptians;
>   and Israel saw the Egyptians dead on the seashore.
>   (V. 30)

All of that is summarized in the assertion, "'That you may know that the LORD makes a distinction between Egypt and Israel'" (11:7). The imagery of chapter 14 is war imagery. God fights for those who cannot defend themselves, not for those who deserve it and might win anyway but precisely for the helpless and worthless because the Lord is with them and for them.

War imagery, when related to God, troubles many people, particularly those who have conventional or "spiritual" notions of religion. But the Lord, the God of the Hebrew Scriptures and Christian Testament, does not fit our religious conventions. We cannot go from our stereotypes to God, but must begin with God and from that understand what the term *God* means. God breaks our stereotypes. It is the good news of these war formulae that in the midst of conflicts where we are abandoned, we are safe because of God's commitment to us. This was evident in very primitive war speeches:

> "Hear, O Israel! Today you are drawing near to do battle against your enemies. Do not lose heart, or be afraid, or panic, or be in dread of them; for it is the LORD your God who goes with you, to fight for you against your enemies, to give you victory." (Deut. 20:3–4)

This with-ness and for-ness is in direct, unqualified speech.

In a much more sophisticated way, the same thing is expressed in the Joseph narrative in Genesis. There God's presence is not so obvious and actions are hidden. Nonetheless, the whole narrative of Joseph and his brothers is premised on the conviction that the Lord's rule will bring God's purpose to be. God's action is decisive and will not be thwarted (cf. Gen. 50:20). Thus in Genesis 39, in which Joseph makes his precarious beginning in Egypt, four times comes the refrain:

> The LORD was with Joseph, and he became a successful man. . . . His master saw that the LORD was with him, and that the LORD caused all that he did to prosper in his hands. (Vv. 2–3)
>
> But the LORD was with Joseph. The LORD was with him; and whatever he did, the LORD made it prosper. (Vv. 21–23)

What had been a primitive war assurance now becomes a serene confidence about life that frees Joseph to act with magnanimous power to give life (45:4–8). But even in this urbane setting, it is still the same commitment of the Lord to the people.

Abiding Presence

Another way in which Israel discerned the Lord's desire to be with and for the people was the tradition that *concerns the temple of Jerusalem* as the place where God is especially present. In the songs of Zion in the Book of Psalms, the Lord is known to be present there to the people:

> God is our refuge and strength,
>   a very present help in trouble. . . .
> God is in the midst of the city; it shall not be moved.
>
> (46:1–5)

But even in that song, God's presence is concerned with action, for immediately the song affirms:

> God will help it when the morning dawns.
>
> (46:5*b*)

Zion is said to be God's place of abiding:

> How lovely is your dwelling place,
>   O LORD of hosts!
>
> (Ps. 84:1)

These hymns affirm and enhance the notion of cultic presence of the Lord in this special holy place. But even there, we are not removed from God's active and powerful intervention. The Lord is characteristically not a God who is but who acts. Thus Psalm 46 not only speaks of God's abiding in Zion. Its twofold refrain is about the war god who is Lord of the troops:

> The LORD of hosts is with us;
>   the God of Jacob is our refuge. . . .
> The LORD of hosts is with us;
>   the God of Jacob is our refuge.
>
> (Ps. 46:7–11)

And his action in this Psalm is to disarm the threatening enemy (v. 9).

Such a notion of cultic presence has the intent of assuring free, safe space in which to receive joyous life. That is why Israel's singers delight to live in the safety of this abiding place (Ps. 23:6). Not because it is empty space simply free of threat, but because it is indeed "sanctuary" where worth is guaranteed and dignity is protected. Even in this confidence, God is not a passive object to be adored nor a static presence to be revered. God is always acting and taking initiative, doing on behalf of the people to make their life better. And because the Lord is not only *with* but *for* the people, Israel's life is characterized by confidence:

> As the mountains surround Jerusalem,
>   so the LORD surrounds his people,
>   from this time on and forevermore.
>
> (Ps. 125:2)

There are problems with such a notion of God's presence, and the Bible itself is not unaware of the danger of such an affirmation. There is always a propensity in religion to want to domesticate the Lord's presence and reduce him to a safe fetish. And against this the Bible protests vigorously:

> "But will God indeed dwell on the earth? Even heaven and the highest heaven cannot contain you, much less this house that I have built!" (1 Kings 8:27)

And this assertion of God's freedom is located exactly in the place where Israel is most vigorous in affirming the importance of the Temple. It is the temptation of religion to have God only *with* us. It is the power of the gospel that God not only *abides with* but is *engaged for* the people, doing what they most need but cannot do, namely, to secure their own existence. Thus there is a tension between the warring presence that intervenes and the cultic presence that abides attentively. The two together affirm both a serene assurance and a rugged intrusiveness that tell us who God is with us.

"Fear Not!"

The Lord's presence is expressed in a special form of speech called the "salvation oracle." It seems to be divine speech in response to a prayer of desperation. It always comes rather abruptly and announces that the situation is not what we thought it was, precisely because the Lord is present where we thought he would not be. It is speech that is announced by "Fear not!" The voice of God is precisely where people are terrified. God's word redefines the situation in terms of God's active presence. Where God is, there is mysterious power but it need not produce terror. Rather it produces amazement that even this situation is being dealt with by the power of God (cf. Mark 4:35–41).

This form of speech is used in the tradition of the patriarchs. Each time, it is to give a great promise just when things seemed most helpless:

> "Do not be afraid, Abram, I am your shield; your reward shall be very great." (Gen. 15:1)

> "Do not be afraid; for God has heard the voice of the boy where he is." (21:17)

> "Do not be afraid to go down to Egypt; for I will make of you a great nation there." (46:3)

Characteristically the presence of the Lord to the people is not only affirmed. God does something! Life is changed. God's presence consists in his faithful action to transform life.

This particular form of speech is especially evident in the exilic literature, addressed precisely to those who felt abandoned:

> Have no fear, my servant Jacob, . . .
>> for I am going to save you from far away. . . .
> For I am with you . . . to save you.
>> (Jer. 30:10–11)

> Do not fear, for I am with you,
>> Do not be afraid, for I am your God;
> I will strengthen you, I will help you,
>> I will uphold you.
>> (Isa. 41:10)

Do not fear, for I have redeemed you;
>   I have called you by name, you are mine.
When you pass through the waters, I will be with you.
>   (Isa. 43:1–2)

These texts (cf. 41:13–14; 44:2) more than any others show how powerful is God's presence. Where God is, life is changed, hope is possible, exile is ended.

Indeed the exile is precisely where Israel had most reason to doubt the Lord's presence and to believe it had been abandoned (cf. Isa. 49:14–15; 54:7–8). And it is especially in exile that another formula of covenantal promise is most used:

You shall be my people,
>   and I will be your God.
(Jer. 30:22; cf. 24:7; 31:33; 32:38; Ezek. 36:28; 37:23,27)

We now know, from God's past with Israel, that to be the people's God means to be actively for them in powerful ways. And to be the Lord's people means to permit life to be transformed and renewed by God's intrusive purposes.

That formula means to assert the Lord's presence against all the apparent evidence. Just where God seems most surely absent, these texts affirm God's characteristic will to be with the people and for the people. Israel is always like Jacob who, in a moment of dismay and then surprise, must say: "Surely the LORD is in this place—and I did not know it!" (Gen. 28:16). And in the parallel narrative, God is not only present, but God is with Jacob:

The Lord: "'I will be with you'" (v. 3).

Jacob: "'The God of my father has been with me. . . . Your father has cheated me and changed my wages ten times, but God did not permit him to harm me'" (Gen. 31:4–7).

This history of the Lord *with the people* and *for the people* is surely what comes to full expression in Jesus of Nazareth. The church's doctrine of incarnation, "word become flesh," is not some metaphysical doctrine. It is rather the church's confession that in the radical self-commitment of Jesus to the powerless and worthless of his time, we can discern the full commitment of God to the world in life-giving ways. We are bold to affirm that in Jesus we know fully and unmistakably that God is not only with us but for us.

"Emmanuel, Which Means, 'God with Us'"

Thus the *Christmas announcement* of Jesus is precisely out of the war tradition of the Lord fighting for his people. It is the angel Gabriel who announces his birth (Luke 1:19,26), and it is no accident that the name of Gabriel means "mighty man of war." The birth announcement is the assertion that God is powerfully at work for those who cannot fight their own battles. The coming of Jesus is the Lord radically and powerfully with the people in times of distress to rescue them. Jesus is the means through which God's faithful covenanting is evident to the people (Luke 1:72–74). In the announcement narratives, Jesus is given two names: "'She will bear a son, and you are to name him Jesus, for he will save his people from their sins. . . .

> "'Look, the virgin shall conceive and bear a son,
> 　　and they shall name him Emmanuel,'
> which means, 'God is with us'" (Matt. 1:21–23).

The first name calls to mind the great heroes of Israel who intervened on behalf of this people in time of trouble (cf. the Book of Judges). The second is a quote from Isa. 7:14 concerning the Lord's assurances that the situation of political oppression and historical hopelessness will be inverted.

Jesus' Ministry

From his birth narratives, which are indeed about the with-ness and for-ness of God, we may better understand the ministry of Jesus, for his ministry is doing what is announced in his birth. His ministry is the focus of the Gospel, especially Matthew, Mark, and Luke. They are interested primarily not in who he is but in what he does. Who Jesus is is known only from what he does. And what he does is to be with us and act for us. He brings power to people whose power is faint and low. He brings food to people desperately hungry. He brings healing where disease seemed to rule. He brings life where death was all they could anticipate. Jesus had no magical power. He was rather the central way in which God showed who he was, the rich man who "for your sakes . . . became poor" (2 Cor. 8:9), the full one who for our sake became empty (Phil. 2:6–11), the living one who faithfully laid down his life (John 10:11). To be with another may only be an act of momentary, condescending charity. But to be for another means to be vulnerable in the situation of another, to suffer with and die for, to be subjected to the conditions and risks of another, to have one's person called into question like that of the other (cf. Rom. 5:8). That is God's goodness, unlike the goodness of any other God (cf. Psalm 82). God shows who God is by the capacity to enter into the suffering of others, to be with, to be identified totally with them and not to be helpless there but still for the other with fresh power. No wonder this God is a peculiar God, like whom there is no other!

What God Promises and What He Asks

We conclude with three quite distinct promises showing God's character. First, the Gospel of Matthew places all God's teaching and ministry in an envelope about being with the people. We have mentioned the first of these in 1:21–23. The ending is a perfect counterpart: "'All authority in heaven and on earth has been given to me. Go therefore and make disciples . . . baptizing . . . teaching. . . . And remember, I am with you always, to the end of the age'" (Matt. 28:18–20). God will be with us to the end of the age. It is a promise for time to come. It is our assurance for now. But it is also a mandate to do something because God is for us. That God is for and with us requires a different kind of life and ministry in response.

Paul also lyrically speaks of this strangeness of God. In his most rhapsodical statement, he asks this central question about the faithfulness and fickleness of God: "If God is for us, who is against us?" (Rom. 8:31). After a series of parallel questions, he answers his own question:

> For I am convinced that neither death, nor life, nor angels, nor rulers, nor things present, nor things to come, nor powers, nor height, nor depth, nor anything else in all creation, will be able to separate us from the love of God in Christ Jesus our Lord. (Rom. 8:38–39)

Nothing and nobody can separate us. Nothing can come between God and the people of the Covenant. This is not because we have a religious bias in our life or that we merit anything, but because of God. God wills Covenant. God is with us because it is God's purpose to be and God will not be thwarted. And we rely on that, on this faithful intention to be with us in order to be for us. Remarkably, in such an eloquent passage, Paul must use the war language of the old tradition to say this about the covenant-making God:

> In all these things we are more than conquerors through him who loved us. (Rom. 8:37)

We are more than conquerors because God fights for us.

Finally, the incredible vision of history resolved in Revelation 21 promises all things new. And in the center of that anticipation is this:

> I heard a loud voice from the throne saying,
> "See the home of God is among mortals.
> He will dwell with them as their God;
> they will be his peoples,
> and God himself will be with them."
>
> (Rev. 21:3)

The hope is a repetition of the old exilic hope of Ezek. 37:27–28:

> My dwelling place shall be with them; and I will be their God, and they shall be my people. Then the nations shall know that I the LORD sanctify Israel, when my sanctuary is among them forevermore.

That hope has a double focus: (*a*) presence to them and (*b*) covenant with them. God's commitment is not to a place but to a people who will live in blessed communion with God. The promise of presence in Rev. 21:3 shows that this presence transforms because it makes all things new:

> "He will wipe every tear from their eyes,
> Death will be no more;
> mourning and crying and pain will be no more,
> for the first things have passed away."
>
> (Rev. 21:4)

It is a creation perfectly reconciled. We do not doubt it will be, because we know who God is and God's powerful faithfulness to keep the promise.

Such faithfulness is a scandal (1 Cor. 1:22–25). It violates all our religious conventions, for we prefer a God not so intensely set on us. The scandal is that it seems not to be so, and we do not wish it so, because it destroys the way we would arrange life. It need hardly be said that this good news calls our whole way of existence into question. It questions our reading of public life, for we would like to organize it in ways that violate God's passion and compassion. It also questions our self-perception. If we are indeed "in God's image," then the central task of our life is covenant-making and covenant-keeping. It is a promise both rich and heavy for us to say that finally we shall be like God (1 John 3:2). Thus our central human vocation is to be with brothers and sisters and for brothers and sisters. That is who God is. That is who we are called to be, expected to be, promised to be. It is a strange name for a baby: Emmanuel. It is even a stranger name for a God!

For Reflection and Discussion

1. Think of the person you most want to be present with you in your times of hurt and need.

   Think of times in your life when the presence of someone made a decisive and positive difference. How was that person present? What did he or she do or say that made a difference? What difference did it make?

2. Describe what you think to be the main characteristics of God. How do you know about these? Are these positive or negative? Do they make any difference to you? Do they contradict what you know of the Gospel in the Bible? Do they reflect your mature faith, or might they be childlike or childish notions that may need to grow up?

3. What would it mean if you would believe God is for us? for you? Can God take sides? Would it matter?

Scripture Passages for Meditation

Mark 4:35–41
Mark 8:31–33
Rom. 8:31–39

Comment

The Gospel of Mark has a "messianic secret." That is, every time somebody discerns who Jesus is, he requires that it be kept a secret. Perhaps it is a secret to this early congregation because in the empire it is too dangerous. (It is still too dangerous to let it be known in our urban world.) More likely it is a secret because he is a strange riddle that violates our reason. He is at the same time the utterly powerful one and the totally powerless one.

In Mark 4:35–41, he is incredibly powerful and acts on behalf of his disciples, the church. They are in danger and have no resources, but because they are with Jesus they are safe. He is with them and for them and that is enough. Even though he is for them and with them, they have no faith, do not trust his power, and can hardly believe he is sufficient for them. At the end of the story, they do not make an affirmation. They only ask a stunned question because it is too much for them.

In Mark 8:31–33 by contrast, Jesus announces his power is not for keeping but for losing. His power will be ultimately disclosed in his readiness to suffer. Peter, and with him the whole church, tries to talk him out of it because Peter and the whole church want Jesus to have power like the emperor, who of course is always seen as powerful and never suffering. Jesus is the strange presence of God whose powerlessness is powerful. The totally vulnerable one is the present ruling Lord.

It is such a strange idea. It calls us to completely change our notions of God's presence to us.

There are very likely special connections between Paul (who wrote Romans) and Mark. It is probable that Mark's Gospel represents the special tradition of Paul's theology. In Rom. 8:31–39 Paul has written the most eloquent statement we have about this strange God being for us and present to us. Notice his list of things that cannot separate us from the powerless-powerful one. Can you think of anything else that might separate us?

5

More of the Same Still to Come

The Bible is the memory book for Jews and Christians. It preserves for us the memories that identify us and largely shape how we will experience the present. But the Bible is never a closed book of past events. When it is understood as a finished record only to be recited and recollected, it is betrayed and its dynamic is lost.

The memories of the Bible are not past-oriented but are set toward the future. The central themes of the Bible are directed toward the future because the God of the Bible has made promises to us that will surely be kept. God is oriented to the future—more interested in the promises yet to be kept than in what has already happened among us. The promises God has made (and watches over to bring to fulfillment) do not permit us to engage in fantasy and wishing for an unlimited variety of things in our future. Our past is prevented from being fixed and closed because it surges toward the future. Our future is prevented from being undisciplined and romantic because the past determines the shape of our future and sets the direction of what we may yet expect from God. The Bible presents a delicate interaction between past and future: The past is powered by the future; the future is disciplined and shaped by the past.

The biblical community of faith is invited always to live between such memories and hopes in interaction with one another. When our memories are torn from our hopes, they become settled and fixed and can no longer address us. When our hopes are torn from our memories, they become wild and self-seeking and unreal. The Bible is oriented toward the future, and so we affirm there is *more to come*. But the future is to be after the manner of God's past actions, and so we say it will be *more of the same*. God is faithful, and so we expect God to act in ways characteristic of God's previous actions. When God acts in time to come, we affirm that God will do the same kinds of things as in the past. Thus it follows that to know how God will act in time to come, we must pay close attention to those of his past actions that have been especially valued by the community of faith.

The Bible is a book about the future, about God's promises coming to fulfillment. But it is about a particular future rooted in the promises he has made to his people. In a time of prognosticators and futurologists who try to make good guesses or even scientifically informed predictions, we study God's characteristic actions to know what we may yet trust him to do. Our central data about the future is not about our resources or our policies and programs. Rather it is about who God is and how God acts. Here I suggest three such shapes for God's future acts that come out of God's history with the people.

God Is the Freedom-Giver

The most powerful and decisive action of God in Israel's past is the Exodus event. Israel's history began in the slave brickyards of Egypt where no history seemed possible. Slaves never had history. They were treated in ways that made it difficult to remember and impossible to hope. The Israelites' situation was the least likely place for any history to begin, least of all this history of compassion and power, for brickyards were not normally places for either compassion or power. The life of the folks in the brickyard was characterized by groans of oppression and cries of distress: "The Israelites groaned under their slavery, and cried out" (Exod. 2:23). That is who they were and how it began. But the odd and decisive turn was what *he answered!* "God heard their groaning, and God remembered his covenant with Abraham, Isaac, and Jacob. God looked upon the Israelites, and God took notice of them" (Exod. 2:24–25).

God heard. God saw. God came down. God delivered. And history was transformed (Exod. 3:7–8)! Israel had freedom given precisely in a context where it did not seem possible. It did not seem possible because in all the history of nations and empires there had never been a God like this one, powerful enough to overcome a brick-making empire, compassionate enough to hear the groan of the wretched to whom God owed nothing, concerned enough to intervene to terminate a history of hopeless oppression. But that is what God did. That is who God is. That is what Israel relied on and that is what the Bible is about. It is God's most decisive action and most characteristic way of acting that he repeats again and again.

Since that unexpected moment in which life was radically transformed by the freedom-giver, Israel has understood its own life differently:

1. It has insisted that of all the things its children must know about faith in this God, the most important is this: "We were slaves and now we are free" (Exod. 12:26–27; 13:8,14–15; Deut. 6:20–24). Israel found countless ways to tell this story so that the newer generation would not forget the dramatic gift of freedom and so that it would know what to expect from the future.

2. Since that time, the Exodus has become the prism through which other experiences have been understood. In the Bible, the memory of Exodus, kept alive by passionate and repeated retelling, has let Israel re-experience the event in a special way. Thus the crossing of the Jordan, when a helpless group of riffraff confronted the mighty cities of Canaan, is presented as another Exodus happening when the God of freedom acted decisively against tyranny (Josh. 4:19–24). In the Babylonian exile, the poet announces that a new Exodus from exile will be so great and powerful that the old one can be forgotten (Isa. 43:18–19).

In our own time, the same perception is possible. Exodus is about the great liberation movements of our time. It is about the new freedoms that come in marriages when relations are transformed. It is about the liberation of a child from fear or an older person from bitterness. All of life is discerned differently through the prism of the Exodus.

3. As we are made in God's image, we are called to be freedom-givers after him. We are also called to be "practitioners of liberation" in our own daily round, sensitive to the issues and hurts of those closest to us and in the great public crises of our time. When we do that, we do the work of God's caring power.

4. The Exodus story has become the shape of God's promised future for his people. The church does not know where or when or in what ways God will act. But because God is faithful, we have confidence that God will continue to act as in our past. The future actions of God, like the past actions, will be to give freedom where it is desperately desired but where it seems impossible that it should come. Precisely there God gives freedom.

God Is the Exile-Ender and the Home-Bringer

In 598 and again in 587 B.C.E., the political power of biblical Israel ended and portions of the people were taken into exile in Babylon. They were not harshly treated for the most part, but they felt enormously displaced. They knew in their life a terrible bitterness and deep hatred (Psalm 137), and some concluded either that God had failed or that all of God's promises were now void and empty. The same sense of displacement is pervasive among many people today who have felt the homelessness and alienation of our modern world dominated by urbanization. This seems to evoke rootlessness and a sense of not belonging. Which is to say that the theme of God the exile-ender is not a narrow or archaic interest, remote from folks today.

Homelessness means the refugees and war orphans that public policy has produced. But it also involves those uprooted by urban projects. Moreover it describes those who no longer seem to belong, who are alienated not only from their own group or family, but from their values and finally from a sense of meaning in their own life. Homelessness is a theme that touches most of our personal lives and many of our public issues.

In the exile, the Bible affirms that God does not will the people to be displaced and that God will act to bring them home. God is not only the shepherd who seeks out the lost (Isa. 40:11) but also the powerful warrior who will defeat the exiling agent (Babylon) in order to permit the people to go home (Isa. 40:10). God is powerful and tender, terrifying and gentle. The good news of this literature is that God is aligned against the organization of the world on behalf of the homeless ones who still yearn to go home (cf. Jer. 29:5–14; Ezek. 37:1–14; Isa. 40:3–4; 43:5–6).

The faith of Israel is that exile is not a permanent condition. God wills the people to be settled safely in a world where they are at home politically and economically as well as psychologically and spiritually. From the experience of return from exile, Israel learned that the homecoming that God will give the people is not some heavenly vision. It is a promise about at-homeness in history, about a secure socioeconomic political place where one belongs and is both free and secure. That homecoming is not only in great public events but in every place of reconciliation. The actions of Jesus are home-bringing events. He came especially to the outcasts, displaced, and rejected ones in society (the lepers, the demon possessed, the sick, the lame). And he acted toward them in ways so that they could be "at home" again (cf. Mark 5:19).

To bring people home is God's work. But it is work entrusted to us. We are also called to deal with the homelessness of our time. That means to transform public institutions that are a part of the alienating process. But it also means caring intervention in people's lives to end estrangement and to give people a sense of belonging. It is a whole new self-understanding to know that our vocation is to end exile and bring people to a sense of being home.

This experience has given vitality to the biblical hope that God will not quit until all the people are at home in the kingdom. This means, until all people know the joy, security, and freedom of living under God's rule. We are, all of us, "seeking a homeland" like father Abraham (Heb. 11:14). We do not doubt that God will keep the promise to create a new history of justice, freedom, and righteousness. God is an exile-ender and finally will end the fractures and alienations of our history.

God Is the Life-Bringer

That is what Israel means to confess in its stories of creation, that God has the power and the will to turn chaos to creation and empty darkness to vibrant light, to deal with the forces of death, and to bring life. And God does this, not by magic or by mystification, but by a powerful lordly word that calls into being creatures designed to listen and answer and to live in faithful covenant with God's self. God is precisely the one who has the authority to call "into existence the things that do not exist" (Rom. 4:17).

It is especially in Jesus that God the life-bringer is evident. Particularly in the story of Easter is life granted to a world of death. The events of Good Friday were the last desperate effort of death to have its way with Jesus. Embodied in civil structures, the power of death caused its moment of darkness and its time of earthquake (Mark 15:33–38). But it could not finally have its way because the life-bringer raised the dead Jesus and in him created an alternative for his entire creation. In the risen Jesus, the church came to know that the power of death is not the only possible conqueror. There is one who is stronger (Mark 3:21–27).

But Jesus as the presence of the life-bringer in a world of death is known not only in the resurrection. Each of his actions is shaped as the triumph of life over death. So he dealt with Zacchaeus, as good as dead, and restored him to joyous life (Luke 19:1–10). He told the story of the son restored to the father, the one who ""was dead and is alive"" (Luke 15:24). He had compassion on the hungry crowds and by feeding them brought life where hunger had held sway (Mark 8:1–10). Indeed, he not only gives life but he redefines it in terms of joyous obedience to the father and joyous caring for the brother and sister. He manages to invert definitions so that what the world had thought was the way to death is the celebrative gift of life and what the world calls life he showed to be deathly existence. So he calls into question all the coercive arrangements that squeeze the life out of God's creation (Matt. 23:1–36).

In response to a question by John, he summarizes all his actions as life-giving: "'The blind receive their sight, the lame walk, the lepers are cleansed, the deaf hear, the dead are raised, the poor have good news brought to them'" (Luke 7:22).

The words must be read both as concerning individual persons in their various disabilities, as well as concerning the transformation of institutions. Thus the good news to the poor is the change of those institutions that have denied them. But it also means a caring gesture. The life-bringing activity of Jesus never lets one choose between public transformation and personal compassion. We are called to do both. And when we do, we bring life. Only in the context of the promises of God are we granted the immense vocation of bringing life into a world where death seems the common venture.

And since then the church has known about the future and has known that God's coming actions would be of the same kind as those God has already done. What God has already done is call into question all the ways we commonly desire and perceive reality. And what God is yet to do will call into question all our allegiances to keep the world the way it is. There is more to come, and it will be as radically shattering and as radically healing as the "mighty works" of God we remember.

The Good News of Jesus

So we have these three motifs that embody our best memories and our deepest hope:
- the freedom-giver
- the exile-ender and home-bringer
- the life-bringer

1. The church has come to see that each of these themes is an accurate characterization of Jesus, of who he was and what he did. *He did give freedom* to the demon-possessed who were locked into their hopeless possession. He also gave it to the poor who were locked forever into debt slavery. *He did end exile,* as he came to lepers and the despised lowly and restored them to power and to a sense of joyful belonging. *He did bring life,* both in his dramatic Easter moment, and in the

way in which he daily did his ministry. In all three ways, he rescued the hopeless, restored them to history, bestowed on them power, and invited them to God's future. Clearly Jesus is a bringer of the newness of God into a weary world that did not expect it and that did not welcome it when it came.

2. The church has learned that these actions disclosed in Jesus are not unique acts but they are characteristic ways of acting. So we may count on more of the same. God will keep on doing what he has done.

His actions are not ended with the Bible. Nor are they stopped by the church that seems at times fickle and immobilized. In his ways, known to us and unknown, by visible heroes and nameless saints, inside the church and outside, he does his work. And we have confidence, not because of progress we make or because of signs we can see, but because we know he is faithful. He keeps at his tasks. And his work continues even in our own time. He is persistent and finally will work his will among us, even when we do not notice or when we choose to resist. He is faithful even when we find it hard to be so.

3. These ways known in Jesus and known also all through God's history with the people are also the shape of biblical hope. Of course we do not know the future. And we do not limit God's freedom or preclude the divine will. But we do know God to be faithful to promises and to past actions. And so God's actions toward us and all creation in the future will be actions to bring about a world according to the sacred purposes, over which God can joyously rule. God's future promise to us is to bring this world more fully to the divine intent. And we know from Jesus and from our whole history that God wills *freedom, at-homeness,* and *life.* God has sworn unending hostility to *slavery, exile,* and *death,* and will not rest until the divine rules over all. Our memory lets us live by the hope that

> "The kingdom of the world has become the kingdom of
>   our Lord
>   and of his Messiah,
> and he will reign forever and ever."

(Rev. 11:15)

4. Jesus' past actions and our future hopes from him define our present ministry. In the context of our memories of him and our promises from him, we live our vocation. We do so in the confidence that his characteristic actions are not ancient dreams or forgotten promises. They are also his present actions. Even now in big and little ways, he frees, he brings home, he gives life. And by that conviction we are powered as his faithful church to do his work with him. That is what our common life is about.

His faithful actions are good news, because they finally will bring us to be whom we are destined to be, namely, his faithful, joyous covenant partners, enjoying his *freedom, at home* in his presence, affirming his *life* to us. That's the Gospel. It concerns whom we and the whole world may yet become because he is faithful to his promises among us:

> But to all who received him, who believed in his name, he gave power to become children of God. (John 1:12)

> Beloved, we are God's children now; what we will be has not yet been revealed. What we do know is this: when he is revealed, we will be like him, for we will see him as he is. (1 John 3:2)

We can live under promises, those promises. It makes a difference now.

For Reflection and Discussion

1. Describe someone whom you judge to be really free. What are the dimensions of freedom in that life?
   - How did that person get free?
   - How does that person stay free?
   - Does freedom have anything to do with political, economic power? Can you be free with it?
   - Does freedom have anything to do with faith, or does faith enslave?
   - Does freedom imply freedom from suffering? or capacity to suffer?
2. Think of the forms of exile in your life or in the lives of persons you know. What causes people to be homeless? What

causes people to be at home? Do you know people who appear to be "at home" but are really homeless? Do you know people who appear to be homeless but are "at home"?

3. Think about the oppressed people of our time—whom would you include? blacks? poor people? old people? women? disabled people? prisoners? It is said by many theologians that God is peculiarly at work among the poor on their behalf. What do you think of that? What would a God of the oppressed do? What might oppressed people hope for? To whom do you think God's promises are given?

Scripture Passages for Meditation

Mark 5:1–20
Eph. 2:11–22

Comment

Consider the man in Mark 5:1–20. He is not a single individual, but a model for every person to whom Jesus comes. He is described in his state of slavery and exile in verses 3–5. Would you call him enslaved? Is he exiled to the cemetery? How did it happen? How are people made into exiles? Is it strange that this exile is the one who immediately recognizes Jesus (v. 6) while more established, safer people resisted Jesus and could not tell who he was?

Jesus does his healing work, and the man is restored to sanity (v. 15). His slavery has ended. This fragmentation is overcome (cf. v. 9). And he is sent home (v. 19). The early church remembered this event because it is the story of every person called to discipleship. In our special need, we can recognize the suffering power of Jesus. The early church under imperial Rome must have felt fragmented and exiled and desperate. But they knew that only by the power of God could their estrangement be transferred to *Rome*. Jesus deals with the deep homesickness of people on the brink of insanity.

In Eph. 2:11–22, Paul describes alienation and asserts that our alienation has been dealt with. We are now not aliens but citizens (v. 19). Believers living in a strange world—either the ancient Hellenistic world or our contemporary one—might be the only ones who are "at home." And that's because God keeps promises.

6

Turn and Live!

The call to conversion is central to the Bible. It is rooted in the conviction that God will not leave us or the church or creation as they presently are, but that a radical newness is possible and is promised by God for those who will receive it. In other words, the central dynamic of the Bible understands life as the double process of *turning loose* from the way things are and *embracing* in great risk the way God has promised they will be. It is, then, the reorientation of life through a fresh central loyalty around which other loyalties and perceptions can be freshly organized.

Conversion and the correlative idea of *repentance* must never be understood in a vacuum. Taken alone, conversion might be reduced to a moralistic idea of accepting some new rule or discipline for life that lacks the power to transform. Or it may be taken as an emotional experience (e.g., the "sawdust trail") that does not substantively affect life commitments and that has no staying power.

Conversion—Entering into Covenant with God

Rather conversion, as it is understood in the Bible, is an act of *entering into covenant* with a new covenant partner. This means coming under a new set of demands. But it also means entering into a different history, embracing a different memory, and living with different promises. And from that, of course, comes a new perceptual world and a new lifestyle so that life is discerned in new ways and one lives, in response, in a very different way. It follows that conversion is not finally something that happens to an individual; it is the formation of a new community powered by a new loyalty. The central converting action in the Bible is the formation of a new community that lives in covenant with the Lord, this God like whom there is no other.

The history of the Lord's call to conversion is the history of forming Israel and of forming the church in which the *ecclesia* (the assembly of the faithful) is gathered from other places and loyalties. Thus covenant-forming by Moses and Joshua is the initiation of the conversion process in the Bible:

> "Now therefore, if you obey my voice and keep my covenant, you shall be my treasured possession out of all the peoples. Indeed, the whole earth is mine, but you shall be for me a priestly kingdom and a holy nation." (Exod. 19:5–6)

> Hear, O Israel: The LORD is our God, the LORD alone. You shall love the LORD your God with all your heart, and with all your soul, and with all your might. (Deut. 6:4–5)

> So now, O Israel, what does the LORD your God require of you? Only to fear the LORD your God, to walk in all his ways, to love him, to serve the LORD your God with all your heart and with all your soul, and to keep the commandments of the LORD your God and his decrees that I am commanding you today, for your own well-being. (Deut. 10:12–13)

> Choose life so that you and your descendants may live. (Deut. 30:19)

> "Now therefore revere the LORD, and serve him in sincerity and in faithfulness; put away the gods that your ancestors served beyond the River and in Egypt, and serve the LORD. Now if you are unwilling to serve the LORD, choose this day whom you will serve, whether the gods your ancestors served in the region beyond the River or the gods of the Amorites in whose land you are living." (Josh. 24:14–15)

These summons invite people to enter covenant and become Israel. And that call means an *abandonment* of other loyalties, a reliance on other means, an embrace of another destiny. Conversion, the decision to be God's holy people, is the *entry* into an alternative consciousness that distances itself from the ways of the culture in which it is placed. The extended traditions of the Torah (Exodus to Deuteronomy) are an attempt to give form and substance to that alternative existence with Yahweh.

Conversion—Both Communal and Personal

It is especially the prophets of Israel, who lived five hundred years after Moses, who most vigorously call Israel to conversion. By that time the people of God had become thoroughly encultured. They lived by the norms and values of their Canaanite environment. The prophets call for a fresh embrace of their covenant with the Lord, insisting that this covenant is a workable form of life, even in the context of urban imperialism. Thus Amos for example:

> Seek me and live. . . .
> Seek the LORD and live. . . .
> Seek good and not evil. . . .
> Hate evil and love good,
>   and establish justice in the gate.
>
> (Amos 5:4–15)

And this is echoed by Isaiah, his contemporary:

> Wash yourselves; make yourselves clean;
>   remove the evil of your doings
>   from before my eyes;
> cease to do evil,
>   learn to do good;
> seek justice,
>   rescue the oppressed;
> defend the orphan,
>   plead for the widow.
>
> (Isa. 1:16–17)

Hosea, their near contemporary, is less precise ethically but makes essentially the same call:

> Sow for yourselves righteousness;
>   reap steadfast love;
>   break up your fallow ground;
> for it is time to seek the LORD,
>   that he may come and rain righteousness upon you.
>
> (Hos. 10:12)

> But as for you, return to your God,
>   hold fast to love and justice,
>   and wait continually for your God.
>
> (Hos. 12:6)

It is evident from these statements that conversion is not something confined to a spiritual or private agenda. Rather a decision is called for that has urgent political and economic implications. The prophets believe that all of life, including public institutions, can be reoriented so that they serve the purposes of the Lord to whom Israel has made covenant vows. The transformed life of Israel, in contrast to the dominant values around them, focuses on justice and righteousness and steadfast love, that is, on compassion for the weak, on fidelity to human persons, and on the ordering of life that transcends self-aggrandizement and self-securing.

In a later text, but one related to these, Joel makes a most radical call to conversion:

> Return to me with all your heart,
> with fasting, with weeping, and with mourning;
>   rend your hearts and not your clothing.
> Return to the LORD, your God,
>   for he is gracious and merciful,
> slow to anger, and abounding in steadfast love,
>   and relents from punishing.
>
> (Joel 2:12–13)

That text, familiar to us for its use in the Lenten season, asserts that a mere change of external appearances is not adequate. What is to be converted is the heart. However, that may not be understood simply as an internal experience. The heart represents in biblical psychology the organ of decision-making through which a life-orientation is determined. Thus the prophet rejects both mere externality in change (garments) and also mere internality that does not make any visible difference. He calls his people to remake the decision of basic commitment that establishes patterns of perception, value, and behavior. The prophets are firm and urgent in calling God's people to live their life, personal and corporate, in terms of the purposes of bringing about justice, righteousness, and faithfulness.

At Once a Human Task and God's Work

These texts set conversion as a human task and so it surely is. But the Bible is also realistic about what human persons are able to do by willpower. It knows that we get so enmeshed in habit and vested interest that we cannot change even if we will to. As Israel's history moves toward exile, the poets become aware that Israel is unable to repent (Jer. 13:23; cf. Rom. 7:19–24). The texts are no less interested in and concerned for conversion than the older voices of the tradition. But they know it must come another way. If there is to be newness, it must have another source. So we may note two remarkable suggestions in this regard.

First, Ezekiel has a fresh idea. He lived in a period of keen discouragement in the exile when no future seemed possible. He called for repentance in vigorous ways (cf. Ezekiel 18), but he knew it was not possible. And so he describes the Lord as prepared to take a radical step, to give Israel new organs of decision-making that could replace the old ones that have now become dysfunctional:

> I will give them one heart, and put a new spirit within them; I will remove the heart of stone from their flesh and give them a heart of flesh, so that they may follow my statutes and keep my ordinances and obey them. Then they shall be my people, and I will be their God. (Ezek. 11:19–20)

> A new heart I will give you, and a new spirit I will put within you; and I will remove from your body the heart of stone and give you a heart of flesh. (Ezek. 36:26; cf. 18:31; 37:14)

The covenant depends now not on the turning of Israel but the gift of a new possibility worked by the Lord himself. When the old organ fails, an organ transplant is envisioned. Thus conversion is not only a work required by God's people, but it is a work of God who freshly equips the people for a reorientation. Conversion is possible because God empowers it.

Second and even more radical, when there is a dysfunction between the Lord and the people and a fracture is unavoidable, when Israel is called to repent and cannot, the *Lord repents*. There is no more radical idea than this in the entire Bible. God is presented not primarily as all-knowing, all-powerful, or all-present but as a covenant partner who freely makes intervention and fresh decision toward the covenant partner. God is in this respect unlike any other God (cf. Exod. 15:11). God is not a static object or a passive entity, but, on the contrary, a dynamic covenant partner who in faithful compassion can act in various ways to renew and transform. The radical announcement of the Bible is that God's self is converted on behalf of the people.

Hosea expressed this most poignantly. After a sharp and abrasive reprimand to his people in Hos. 11:1–7, there seems no way out. The covenant is over. Israel is so turned from the Lord that it is unwilling, even incapable, of returning to covenant. But God so wills the relation that God acts. God is converted to a new way:

> My heart recoils within me;
> > my compassion grows warm and tender.
> I will not execute my fierce anger;
> > I will not again destroy Ephraim;
> for I am God and no mortal,
> > the Holy One in your midst,
> > and I will not come in wrath.
>
> (Hos. 11:8–9)

God's "godness" consists not in remote indifference but in passionate freedom to sustain the relation with the people.

In Amos the same note is sounded. Amos prays to the Lord on behalf of Israel, interceding that God not act in justifiable wrath against Israel. And God is moved by the prayer:

> The LORD relented concerning this;
>> "It shall not be," said the LORD.
>
> (7:3,6)

The narrative of Jonah is parallel:

> When God saw what they did, how they turned from their evil ways, God changed his mind about the calamity that he had said he would bring upon them; and he did not do it. (3:10)

This verse expresses a double conversion, Nineveh to God and God to Nineveh. The notion of the Lord's capacity to repent affirms both deep, divine compassion and God's extraordinary freedom to act according to the sacred purposes and not according to any preordained rule or stereotype. Such a motif suggests to us the profoundly covenantal and deeply personal character of the Lord. The Lord is not like any other god in the world, ancient or modern. And the Lord will not fit conventional religious notions. God wills covenant, insists on the people turning to the Lord, but asks nothing of them that God's self will not do. God turns to the people. God is radically *for* the people. And it is God's turning that makes their turning possible. Such a surprising notion of God yields a remarkable understanding of humanness, for we are "made in God's image." It announces that our mature humanness consists in the capacity to repent, in our willingness to care so deeply and to change so freely that we can make vows and keep them. In our doing this, we are most like the God who has created us and continually calls us to God's self.

Bad News and Good News

The theme of conversion, of course, is no less central in the Christian Testament. It is widely agreed that a call to repent is the central teaching of Jesus. This is what he came to say first, and it may well be the core of all that he had to say: "'The time is fulfilled, and the kingdom of God has come near; repent, and believe in the good news'" (Mark 1:15). This announcement has three parts: (*a*) the call to repent, to enter a new arrangement;

(*b*) the empowerment to repent found in the good news; and (*c*) the substance of repentance is positive and not negative. It is not to leave but to enter, not to give up but to embrace the new arrangement. Too often talk about repentance is done without good news and without the positive invitation to an alternative. Jesus is not a teacher of a new morality, either more rigorous or more permissive. He is the proclaimer and bringer of a new age in which the claims of old power relations have lost their force and in which the joyous rule of God has begun to be fulfilled. It is good news that we live where God rules, and this new age invites us to new ways of life. Jesus appeals not only to individuals; he announces that a whole order has lost its power. People need no longer spend their lives serving loyalties and values that demand and destroy but do not have the power to give life. He believed and showed that consent may be withdrawn from the order of the old age because the old arrangements have lost their credibility.

Jesus' announcement of a new possibility and the urgency of choosing it is expressed in two forms to two elements of society. On the one hand, he carries on a ministry to well-off people who had long ago settled in and presumed that God's good rule was already present in the ordering that blessed them so well. To these Jesus exposes the distorted and partial quality of such existence and invites people to abandon it (Mark 10:17–22). Indeed in every way he announced that the oldness is over and must be given up. To such people conversion means letting go of an arrangement that benefits them at the expense of others. Such a call to conversion is a harsh demand that old compromising ways be terminated. Obviously this is bad news. It is the embodiment of what the Christian Testament means by crucifixion, of declaring in our life that the deathly ways of the old age have no power over us and that we can reject them. This is what Jesus did that Friday and what he calls his people to do with him.

But Jesus' call to conversion is also good news. It is bad news to those who crave the old order. It is good news to those neglected by the old order who desperately yearn for newness that cannot be any worse and surely will be better. The ones neglected by the old order obviously include the poor and those denied a fair share of the well-being of the community.

But in a society based on competence, the rejected can also be those who succeed in the system but are exploited and dehumanized by the system. They also are finally made powerless even though they manage the system itself. To those Jesus gave power. By his presence, his word, and his incredible actions, he inaugurated a new power arrangement no longer interested in coveting, control, and manipulation but consisting in freely given gifts. The old age that people are called to leave is a righteousness based on law that measures and rewards everything by goodness, obedience, competence, and success. The New Age that people are called to enter is based on a new righteousness that comes from God, which is freely given and for which there are no preconditions for qualification (Rom. 10:1–5). The New Age is evident, for example, in the event of Mark 2:1–12 in which Jesus heals and forgives. And he taunts them by saying, "Should I heal or forgive?" And they want neither because by doing so he declared that their notions of sickness had lost their power and their notions of guilt were now irrelevant. And the power of that new definition of reality permitted the man to go home. "Home" is a powerful image in the Bible and in our time. We are of course aware of the pathos of displaced persons. But Peter Berger has shown how the whole society is organized to keep people "homeless," that is, living so that life is never coherent or integrated. Many people, then and now, are not poor but they are alienated so that they do not belong anywhere. And the good news is that displaced persons are empowered to belong, to have both dignity and security! To do so, Jesus must expose the exile-producing powers of culture. It is no wonder people were amazed; they had defined the situation so that no newness was even thinkable. And now it had come! It had come because the Kingdom comes where he brings it. Amazement is the appropriate response when God's newness overcomes our arrangements.

The ministry of Jesus is to bring people to decide between these two ways of organizing life. He requires that they should choose between them, although the choice he offered caused people terror and amazement. Some were terrified because they clung desperately to the old ways. And some received gladly because the newness was welcome to them. They were the ones who experienced not only *the crucifixion of abandoning* what

is old but also the *resurrection of receiving* the surprising newness of God. Both those who were terrified and those who were
amazed had their characteristic reactions: "The chief priests, the
scribes, and the leaders of the people kept looking for a way to
kill him; but they did not find anything they could do, for all the
people were spellbound by what they heard" (Luke 19:47–48).

The Gift of New Hearts

These issues are not outworn or superseded, whether we are
talking about the church or society, about personal decisions or
public questions. It is whether to live toward the gods of coercion that enslave and alienate or toward the God of freedom
and reconciliation who makes all things new. It is not a churchy
decision but has to do with the loyalties we embrace, the tasks
we accept, the values we serve and fear. Those who cling to
the old age under the conviction that God is not really in
charge are called "hard of heart" (Mark 3:5; 8:17). The teaching
of Jesus is not naive or romantic. It does not suggest that conversion is easy. In fact it is "impossible" (Mark 10:27). But the
good news is precisely that this impossibility is wrought among
such as us by the power of God. The good news is that hard
hearts are displaced by new hearts and that new hearts can receive the new righteousness from God. That is a more won-
drous gift than most of us can imagine, but it is what conversion
is about.

The question Israel had to face was which God to serve
(cf. Josh. 24:14–15). That is still the question that the church
must face. The world is organized as though other powers are
really ultimate. The church is often lured into such loyalties, and
then the good news is neither credible nor powerful. Repentance does not lead to the Gospel, but it is the good news that
liberates us enough to believe the Gospel. God is at work both
urging and empowering our conversion.

For Reflection and Discussion

1. The Good News of the Gospel is that the world does not
   need to be organized the way it is. How do you think the

world is organized? How is power distributed: at home? in school? at work? How did it get that way? Who wants to keep it that way?

2. The Good News is that God has already organized the world in a new way, even though it still appears to be organized in old ways. How do you think God has willed the world to be reorganized? Do you see any evidences of it?

3. Reorganizing the world means distributing power differently:
   • Name people who have power but use it in destructive ways.
   • Name people who, according to the Gospel, ought to have more power than they have.
   • According to the Gospel, what kind of power do you have that might need to be reorganized?
   • According to the Gospel, what kind of power might be given to you that you don't now have or even want?

4. Repentance means accepting God's new ordering of the world and living in it even though it isn't widely recognized. What would such repentance mean for you? Would it involve some risks? Would it involve some actions that seem risky?

Scripture Passages for Meditation

Luke 1:51–55
Luke 14:12–14

Comment

Here are two texts from Luke that speak of repentance in most radical times. The Christian community that Luke served had a particular sensitivity to the poor. It believed God was especially attentive to and concerned for the poor. It believed that God would intervene and radically *invert* the flow of power.

In 1:51–55, Mary is remembered as singing about God's very old promise to Abraham and Sarah, a promise that God would make things new especially for the hopeless. In her song, Mary speaks of the high become low and the low become high. Not only are the hungry fed but the well-off do not eat. That poem suggests a reading of our life with God that is very hard to take, especially if we are well off.

And the little teaching of 14:12–14 also is about repentance. It calls us to abandon a quid-pro-quo world in which everything is a trade-off and to enter a new world of unconditional gift.

We can read that in terms of social policy. But we can also read it in terms of changing our inner life to new kinds of joy and freedom. Repentance is not about all kinds of petty things. Rather it concerns life in God's world of remarkable promises. That would really be a "new nature." Clearly Luke's Gospel provides a sharp alternative to Hellenistic cultural views of Luke's time.

John Swomley, in his book *Liberation Ethics,* asserts that real change happens when a group of people "deny legitimacy" to certain values. It is clear in Luke 14:12–14, Jesus is urging his new community of disciples to "deny legitimacy" to a conventional social practice and assumptions. That's real repentance.

7

"From Death to Life"

Life Means Relatedness

The Bible has notions of life and death that are very different from those we have today. Whereas we think of *life* as the continuing functioning of the individual organism and *death* as the cessation of such functioning, the Bible understands life and death in covenantal categories. *Life* means to be significantly involved in a community of caring, meaning, and action. Death means to be excluded from such a community or denied access to its caring, meaning, or action. *Life* means a capacity to enter into covenants and the ability to make covenants that are also community-creating possibilities for others. Life and death do not have to do, in biblical perspective, simply with the *state of the individual person* but with the *relation between the person and the community* that identifies that person and that gives personhood. A German scholar, Jungel, has shown that life in the Bible means *relatedness*. Conversely death is to be *unrelated*. Thus the Bible calls into question two of our dominant presuppositions: (*a*) that life is concerned primarily with biological functioning and (*b*) that life concerns a personal unit in and of itself.

The central life-death moment in the biblical perspective is entry into and participation in a community of identity and mission. *Birth* is *embrace of covenant community,* whether we speak of birth or rebirth. And *death* is *departure from that community,* either by force or by choice. Thus to choose life or death (Deut. 30:19) means to decide upon relationship for or against the life-giving community.

In the Hebrew Scriptures, such an embrace of life means incorporation into the covenant community whereby people are invited in and take vows of allegiance and oaths of fidelity (Exod. 24:1–8; Josh. 24:1–28). In the Christian Testament, such a dramatic, intentional act is likely to be identified with baptism, which means putting off an old nature and coming to life in a new nature (Eph. 4:1–24). The community of meaning and destiny thus has it within its power to give life and consign to death. In the earliest community this had to do with the pronouncement of blessings and the declaration of curses (especially Leviticus 26 and Deuteronomy 28). While this may strike us as primitive, it is psychologically and sociologically correct, given a biblical understanding of personhood, that life is the experience of being identified with community and that death means exclusion, banishment, excommunication. The key issue is relationship, and the primal events are dramatic (liturgic) acts of inclusion and exclusion. While this sounds alien to us, the same dynamic is clearly operative for a teenager who does not get included in a peer group, a young person not chosen for a team, a small child rejected by a parent. The breaking of a significant relationship is an experience of death.

Life Is a Task

The Bible regards life and death as a two-sided issue. And the two sides must be kept in careful tension with each other. On the one hand, life is a task. It is a work that is assigned to a community and that the community must intentionally undertake. If the community quits on the task, the community disintegrates and there will be death. Perhaps it is the coming of this kind of death that we are experiencing in America today because we have not regarded life as a task that the national community must address. The prophets of Israel in the eighth and seventh centuries B.C.E. were most articulate about such a situation. The Israelites in that period were secure and complacent and took everything for granted. Not unlike ourselves, they presumed upon the pride and affluence they saw everywhere. They concluded that it would never end and was eternally guaranteed. It is the prophets who announce to the community of meaning and destiny that life never just happens. It requires sustained, disciplined effort to enhance and continually reform the community. The kings of Israel, prototypes of those who forgot the task of life, turned out to be the agents of death, that is, the cause of the unrelatedness that leads to disintegration.

The prophet Amos issues such a call to life as a task:

> Seek me and live. . . .
> Seek the LORD and live. . . .
> Seek good and not evil. . . .
> Hate evil and love good,
>   and establish justice in the gate.
>
> (Amos 5:4–15)

The task of securing life means to turn away from all other loyalties except to the Lord, the God of the Bible. It requires sharing his vision and rejecting every other vision of what community can be. Concretely it means to seek "good," which is the well-being for all members of the community, and to establish justice; that is, to care for the weak and powerless, to give sustenance to the helpless. It means to orient and reorganize public institutions so that the weak and powerless are not excluded as unqualified. These are the tasks of *life* in ancient Israel and in every community. Isaiah echoes the task in a series of imperatives:

> Wash yourselves; make yourselves clean;
>   remove the evil of your doings
>   from before my eyes;
> cease to do evil,
>   learn to do good;
> seek justice,
>   rescue the oppressed,
> defend the orphan,
>   plead for the widow.
>
> (Isa. 1:16–17)

When these tasks are not embraced, death surely comes (cf. Amos 5:1–2).

Life Is a Gift

The other side of the tension is that *life is a free gift.* In the sixth century B.C.E., two hundred years after Amos and Isaiah, Israel was no longer proud and secure. Now its institutions had collapsed and its nerve had failed. It now doubted whether sustained life was possible. Perhaps we are on the edge of such doubting in our society. Disintegration seemed very near to Israel. There was (and is) a frantic tendency to want to prop things up and, by being a bit more ingenious, to keep things going. But to no avail.

The prophets in the sixth century asserted the radical notion that a community cannot manipulate life because it is a gift from God, and God has not placed the gift of life at our disposal. That is a warning for every community that takes itself too seriously or values its own resources too highly. So Ezekiel announces that life for this community of despair is a free gift from God:

> "They say, 'Our bones are dried up, and our hope is lost; we are cut off completely.' . . . Thus says the Lord GOD: I am going to open your graves, and bring you up from your graves, O my people; and I will bring you back to the land of Israel. And you shall know that I am the LORD, when I open your graves, and bring you up from your graves, O my people. I will put my spirit within you, and you shall live, and I will place you on your own soil. (Ezek. 37:11–14)

The prophet uses resurrection imagery to speak of restoration of the community and rehabilitation in a land of well-being and security. It is pure gift. It is new life in renewed relations.

And his later contemporary also announced to exiles (lost, excluded, dead) that life is a free gift:

> Ho, everyone who thirsts,
>   come to the waters;
> and you that have no money,
>   come, buy and eat!
> Come, buy wine and milk
>   without money and without price.

Why do you spend your money for that which is not bread,
and your labor for that which does not satisfy?
Listen carefully to me, and eat what is good,
and delight yourselves in rich food.
Incline your ear, and come to me;
listen, so that you may live.

(Isa. 55:1–3)

It is the continuing task of maturing for every faith community to embrace both realities that *life is task* and that *life is free gift*. Unless they are kept in balance, either we will be complacent people who are cynical in presuming too much, or we will be weary people who exhaust ourselves to no avail. The choice between cynicism and exhaustion is not an inviting one because both are forms of death.

Death and Resurrection

Jesus is the presence of God who came to put the question of life and death to God's people. He is a bringer of news, but it is both bad and good news. He pronounces good news to those who thought life was a hopeless task, telling them that it is a free gift. He does this to the disenfranchised and powerless: the lepers, the demon-possessed, the poor, all those who were outcasts, whom the community had banished and in fact declared dead. The resurrection power of Jesus is not some magic trick of coming out of the tomb; it is his authority to include back in the community of meaning and destiny those who false authority had declared dead because they did not qualify for life. Thus, for example, he meets a man consigned to life among the tombs, for society has pronounced a death sentence over him (Mark 5:2). Jesus has the power to restore him to life and sends him home. The story ends with his empowerment and restoration (Mark 5:19). Again the *home* motif is at work. The essential estrangement of humanity is a major premise of a biblical understanding of human personality. The homelessness requires an awareness of our essential alienation, but also an alert social criticism to discern how our spiritual alienation is reflected in and embodied by our institutional forms.

But Jesus the life-bringer also brought bad news. He had a different ministry to those who counted too much on the way things were. They had settled in and presumed life was an enduring gift that need only be protected and coveted. To these Jesus announced that life is a demanding task that must be addressed. They thought they were the flower of life, but he declares them to be tombstones (Matt. 23:27–28) and calls them to the task of life. He uses such hard and abrasive imperatives as repent and "bear good fruit" (Matt. 7:16–20).

The story of Jesus' "passion," that is, his history of pathos, suffering, and caring on the way to his cross, is the story of being in the crunch between the gift and the task. He is in hard conflict with those who refuse the task of life and count on a free gift. He is identified with the poor and powerless who cannot perform the task and are denied the gift. His crucifixion on Friday is his exclusion from the community. He is banished by the authorities, killed outside the city as a despised reject. The powers of death, that is, the powers of exclusion, banishment, and denial, have their powerful way. They are the agents of deep fear, for death is often an agent of fear.

But the other motif is the coming of Jesus again to the church on Easter. The early Christians were not much interested in the mechanics of his coming out of the tomb, but they were mightily moved by his present power to gather outcasts around him to form a new community. Resurrection is the good news that the banished, destroyed one, is the one (the only one) who has the power to create a new community in which the gift of life and the task of life are kept together in a healing balance.

Jesus' presence is a conflict between his love for life in the beloved community and the agents of death who resent his news of life as gift and who reject his news of life as task. Jesus and his people always live between *the banishment of Friday* and *the gathering of Sunday,* always between *the exile of crucifixion* and *the new community of resurrection.* We should not miss the point. He was killed precisely because he showed that unrelatedness is not the will of God and is not the way a society can be ordered. It is the case, then and now, that some people prefer and profit from life organized in that way. Jesus, with another vision, worked toward a *related* community, one powered to life. Of course when he did that, everything had to be re-arranged. Some welcomed such a resurrection and some did not.

The Gospel of Matthew has preserved a remarkable tradition about the resurrection. When news came that Jesus was alive and had not finally been done to death, the guards feared retaliation from the established order. The chief priests and elders proposed this solution: "And if this comes to the governor's ears, we will satisfy him and keep you out of trouble" (Matt. 28:14). Resurrection is recognized as a disturbance to those who like existence organized for deathly unrelatedness. The power of the resurrection is subversive because it calls into question the patterns of death and exclusiveness, the patterns of competence and qualification on which society is organized. Resurrection is the recognition that God so wills life and so forms community that the very ones the world rejects are the ones to whom new life comes. No questions are asked by him about social utility.

What Jesus the life-bringer did supremely in his resurrection, he did in his whole ministry. Thus for example, he receives the paralytic (Mark 2:1–12), the one who was immobilized and had lost his worth. He was by every norm "as good as dead." Jesus deals with him in two ways: (*a*) he forgives sin, that is, he removes the pressure that had immobilized him and made him dead; (*b*) he empowers him to walk. He restores him to life and power. This story, like most of the others, is about the capacity of Jesus to bring life from death, not by being a magician or a miracle worker, but by having the authority to overcome the power of death that is at work in our world.

This power of death shows itself in many ways. It is a spiritual power in the world. But it has social manifestations and characteristically shows itself among those who for reasons of interest do not want newness, cannot tolerate forgiveness (of themselves or others), and cannot accept restoration of the undeserving. Jesus refers to such status-quo persons as hard of heart (Mark 3:5; 6:52; 8:17). Hardness of heart, inability to accept newness, resistance to any healing that is not based on qualifications—these are the main enemies of resurrection as it comes in the presence of Jesus.

The Church Is the Community of Resurrection

The church consists in those who have been dead and are alive. It is the company of those who were banished and are restored, of those who were paralyzed and are forgiven, of those who were immobilized and are empowered to function fully again! (Luke 15:24). That is the free gift of life.

And the church, as the company of the "dead-made-alive," is entrusted with the power and vocation of life-giving in a world organized for death. Acts 3:1–10 is a paradigm for a church engaged in a ministry of resurrection. It is about resurrection as much as the Easter story of Jesus. Peter and John surely embody the church. They come to a lame man who embodies all the lost, dead, banished in the world. So it is a meeting between agents of resurrection and those whom the world has declared dead. There is drama in the narrative because we must always wonder whether the church has the power to invert a condition of death. The apostles have no resources, but that is their power. They are as poor as the poor man Jesus who turned out to have the real power. They have only their presence and their word, like the presence and word of Jesus. But they have the power to enable a man to walk and function again. He is brought back among the living when he had ceased to hope for it. Life comes, and the agent of such new life is the church that here is unworried about resources and survival and well-being. John and Peter in this moment know it is enough to be engaged in the risk of the Gospel, the risk that the power of life entrusted to them is strong enough to overcome the power of death.

It should be obvious by now that life, Gospel-life, is not primarily life beyond death in any conventional sense. Nor is it some spiritual private realm. Rather it concerns the restoration to full power and full function in the total life of the historical community. Resurrection is personal in that individuals are rehabilitated, as is clear in the ministry of Jesus. But resurrection is public because it concerns the restoration and transformation of public institutions for the sake of human well-being. Jesus and the church faithful to his life-giving ministry are always a threat to institutions that are organized toward death.

Our world has become cynical and exhausted so that resurrection seems not likely. But that is because we do not discern either the power of God or the fact that our world is
finally subject to God's power. We have been seduced to expect
something less from the power of God than full entry into our
historical existence. The risen ones are empowered

- to speak a new language
- to sing a new song
- to have a fresh picture of self
- to value brothers and sisters in new ways
- to discern and act upon public issues in fresh and bold ways
- to know the good news of God in ways that matter

The whole Bible concerns people who have been out of
covenant being included back into covenant. Those are especially invited back who seem not qualified. This resurrection
gift of new life is precisely a function of God's radical grace that
includes a dismantling of the structures of exclusion. The new
righteousness of God that brings life calls into question every
other norm of righteousness that leads to death (Rom. 10:1–4).

No wonder God's people have been consistently dazzled
and amazed by the gift of life: "We know that we have passed
from death to life because we love one another. Whoever does
not love abides in death" (1 John 3:14). Resurrection news matters today urgently for the church and for civil society. It is a
free gift to have a brother or a sister to love. It is a joyous task
to love them in ways that heal and transform. Our world is in
love with death. But we know another gospel—about the surprise of life.

For Reflection and Discussion

1. Characterize the life and death dimensions of your own ex-
   istence:
   - What are things that symbolize life for you—which rela-
     tionships, convictions, patterns of behavior?
   - What are the things that make for death in your life—
     which relationships, convictions, patterns of behavior?
2. In what ways are you a death-bringer? a life-bringer?
   - Think of specific ways in which you do the task of life,
     that is, build life-giving relationships.

- Is your life-giving activity open and imaginative? How might it be more effective?
3. Erich Fromm has written about necrophilia, "love of death." Can you think how our schools, government, television, and church foster a love of death? What does it mean that God is a life-lover?

Scripture Passages for Meditation

Ezek. 18:3–32
Mark 8:34–38
Mark 10:17–31

Comment

The early church focused much on the life question. Because of who he was, Jesus had a way of requiring people to face the question. The culture in which the church was situated did not like to think about life because that would also expose the deathly ways in which we live. That culture and ours wish to avoid both the life and the death questions.

Thus the Gospel raises the life question. But it also provides an unexpected answer. The early church (in the person of the rich young man) learned from Jesus that keeping commandments is necessary to life but is not enough. The radical affirmation of Jesus is that keeping equals losing and losing equals saving (Mark 8:35). That is the scandal of the Gospel that violates our best values. Life does not come from all the ways we have tried to save, secure, and protect ourselves. That way lies death. The way to life, that is, full, joyous relations, is in the very way our world thinks death comes. What Jesus taught he also embodied. The way to Easter is Good Friday. The victory of resurrection requires the vulnerability of crucifixion.

That of course is not simply a call to personal piety but a call to new forms of public policy. It is an open question whether a death-loving culture can reorder itself toward life. Of course it is also a question whether it has any serious alternatives. God has no intention that we should self-destruct!

8

"Power to Become Children of God"

The invitation of the biblical God is that persons may enter into covenant with God. They may enter into that covenant not because they are qualified or can do something for God but because God wills covenant (cf. Deut. 7:6–11). In contrast to every other god, God is the one who is willing to make lasting promises and enduring commitments to his covenant partners. The Lord, the God of the Bible, is above all a covenant-making, covenant-keeping God.

When one enters into covenant with this God, one also enters covenant with *his people*. There is no solitary covenant with the Lord; it is always covenant *in a community* of people who have made like commitments and received parallel promises from God. The Christian Testament phrase to be "in Christ" means to be in the community of his covenant:

> But it is God who establishes us with you *in Christ* and has anointed us. (2 Cor. 1:21)

> So if anyone is *in Christ,* there is a new creation; everything old has passed away; see, everything has become new! (2 Cor. 5:17)

> As many of you as were baptized *into Christ* have clothed yourselves with Christ. (Gal. 3:27)

> To the saints and faithful brothers and sisters *in Christ* in Colossae. (Col. 1:2)

Being joined to this God means to be joined to a different community with a distinctive identity and destiny.

It is the belief of the Bible that when one enters this community in covenant with the Lord, it is a decisive change in one's life. It is not joining another organization along with others, or adding another loyalty alongside all the others. Rather it is a sharp reorientation of every loyalty already claiming us.

The action of God in Jesus Christ is God's gift of *"power to become children of God"* (John 1:12). There is no more radical statement in the Scriptures than this. It is the good news that outsiders have been adopted and received into the family of God. This affirmation by John is paralleled by Paul: "If anyone is in Christ [i.e., in the community covenanted to God], there is a new creation: everything old has passed away" (2 Cor. 5:17). Entry into this covenant completely changes the identity of the new person, not because he or she is able to change everything, for none of us can do that, but because there are now new relationships at work that do change everything, even in spite of us.

The new relation, defined by God and not by the joiner, is one of being a precious family member welcomed into the household of faith (Eph. 2:19). That change takes place because God has certified the welcome into the family. It is an act of power, the speaking of a claiming, adopting word that no other can deny. God has the *power to redefine our status in life.* This adoption is in God's power to give, and God wills it for us.

Slaves Become Sons and Daughters

This good news exposes our previous status as one that can and must be given up. We are empowered to quit being who we were. We are permitted to regard ourselves differently. Two images suggest themselves by which we may appreciate what it means to be adopted children. First, before people in the biblical world become adopted and treasured children, they are often slaves or servants. They are already present in the household, but they have no value of their own. They are kept only for the work they can perform. They have no rights and no reason to hope for any long-term security. They do not belong. Indeed their well-being depends completely on their good performance.

The slave motif is at the root of biblical imagery. In the Exodus event, the Lord frees the slaves because the Lord has adopted them as treasured children:

> "Thus says the LORD: Israel is my firstborn son. I said to you, 'Let my son go that he may worship me.'" (Exod. 4:22–23)

In that powerful act of liberating, the slaves' status in life is redefined, and they are given a new identity. They cannot refuse it, and Pharaoh cannot resist it. God has power to make people into God's precious children (cf. Matt. 3:9). Now their life consists not in the capricious pleasures of the brickyard Pharaoh but in the affirming fidelity of this God who takes children into God's household.

Our society is filled with the same kind of slaves, people who must daily establish their worth by performing someone's assigned tasks. These are people who must daily live with anxiety concerning the day when they will be unable to perform. Slaves live by obedient performance, effectively accomplishing what is expected. They are nameless agents without intrinsic worth.

The Lord characteristically transforms slaves into children. This is evident in the story of the prodigal son, Luke 15:11–32. The son came home to be a servant: "'Father, I have sinned against heaven and before you; I am no longer worthy to be called your son; treat me like one of your hired hands'" (15:18–19). But the father will not consider it and makes his own insistence: "'Quickly, bring out a robe—the best one—and put it on him; put a ring on his finger and sandals on his feet. And get the fatted calf and kill it, and let us eat and celebrate; for this son of mine was dead and is alive again; he was lost and is found!'" (15:22–24). The son was welcomed to the father's table of joy, for a son does not gain his worth by his *performance* but by *the will of the father*.

Orphans Become Adopted Children

A second biblical image is that people are orphans—people who belong nowhere, who have no identity or rootage and no claim on anyone or anything. The term *orphan* sociologically refers to those who have no voice in government, no advocate in court, no representation in any decision. They are helpless victims without power to make any decisions about their own life. It is the staggering news of the Bible that the Lord takes orphans and brings them into God's family, declares them God's children, gives them a new identity, and redefines their status: "[God] executes justice for the orphan and the widow, and . . . loves the strangers, providing them food and clothing" (Deut. 10:18). "'In you the orphan finds mercy'" (Hos. 14:3).

Our society is filled with such rootless people. It includes the economically disadvantaged who have no advocate among the powerful. It also includes some powerful who are rootless and in fact belong nowhere. It is a striking reality that lostness and displacedness characterize both the conventional poor who owe their soul to the company store and the beholden class of middle-income people who also are enmeshed in corporate structures that displace. Vance Packard has shown how we are *A Nation of Strangers*. He describes the disintegration of personality and community with such displacement. The Gospel is not only an assurance of belonging but a harsh protest against such an ordering of society.

The good news of adoption is addressed to no special class. Rather it addresses persons of every age and class whose humanity is diminished by displacement. It may be that a perception of reality free of ideology will enable us to see that this is a malady effectively destroying our common notion of humanness. Humanness means to belong and to have dignity! But among us are the demonic powers of alienation that address us all.

Sons and Daughters Have a Future

Slaves and orphans receive a new identity because of the father. They are given a name, not any old name, but a royal name, child of the sovereign. They are invested with royal authority. The empowerment of the father's action is not power to get by but power to have a major voice in their own destiny. As children of the royal household, they not only have a name, they have a future. God characteristically comes to people who can hope for nothing and creates for them a new future in which promises are yet to be kept. So the slaves in ancient Israel could not hope, and God gave them a whole new history. And Jesus came especially to the weary poor and announced a new history for them (Luke 4:18–19). Our society is filled with hopeless people, whether they are the poor who have quit trying or the affluent middle class who are wearied with simply coping. Despair is a pervasive malady among us. We do not believe newness can come. We do not expect to be surprised any more. Only sons and daughters who know and trust the father can hope. These are the ones called "heirs" because they know the father is utterly reliable. He has more gifts to give and more words to speak. Those invited regularly to his presence wait in "eager longing" for that which they will yet receive (Rom. 8:19; cf. Gal. 4:1–7).

Sons and Daughters Have a Vocation

A central issue for the community is this: How will the new sons and daughters of God live their life? The new sons and daughters have received not only a *new identity* and a *new future* but also a *new vocation*. They are called to something new and should have high expectations. *Slaves* never have a vocation, for they are left with daily tasks, each of which is taken by and for itself. *Orphans* never have a vocation, only a floating existence, a staggering for survival finally centered nowhere. In contrast to slaves and orphans, *children* have power to live different lives because they know what the father is doing, what he has done, and what he will yet do. Sons and daughters are privileged to understand the whole career of God, to see the large pattern of what God is up to, and to share in the pattern, flow, and focus of God's history. Identity with the will of the father does not mean keeping a long set of rules or instructions.

It means knowing his purposes so well that we are trusted with many alternatives and much freedom to determine how faithfulness to the purposes of the father can now be advanced.

Our new identity and redefined status as sons and daughters of God include living in "blessed communion" with God, that is, relying on covenant. But it also means doing God's purposes: doing in our life what we have discerned God characteristically doing in our history. The relation between father and children is one of grateful trust. It is not a matter of constraint and coercion, of having to do what the father compels. Rather, it is a full embrace of the visions and dreams of the father so they are appropriated and made their own by the children. The life of the believer and of the church is one of joyous identification with God's own work.

Our Task of Reconciliation

God's own work, now embraced by the filial church, is nothing less than reconciliation (2 Cor. 5:17–18). It grieves the heart of God that the children are estranged from God and from one another. God wills an utterly reconciled community and is at work toward that reality.

1. The task of reconciliation includes *the ordering of the family of faith* itself. It is ludicrous for the beloved sons and daughters of God to be alienated in their own life. Surely at the center of God's vision of reconciliation is an image of a united church. And that will not come by trade-offs or power plays but by a new radical obedience in which our hoped-for unity calls us to abandon much of our divisive history, even that part of it that we treasure.

2. The task of reconciliation means *action of solidarity* with the "little ones," the weak, the poor, the powerless. That is a very hard question for the settled church, for we would rather practice charity toward "them" than solidarity with "them." As God has power to redefine our status, so our ministry is nothing less than the empowerment of other sons and daughters who have until now been denied power. Talk of empow-

erment means the end of "business as usual." It requires the reorientation and redistribution of power.

Reorientation means that we come to *think in new ways about power,* not as a means of security and control, but as a way of participation and communion. Much of the power we have come to possess and crave is power *over others.* We have some radical rethinking to do about power *with others.* And we can learn this only by studying the power of Jesus, for he exercised no power over brothers and sisters but was perceived as having great authority. He had the remarkable capacity to *empower* because he made himself *vulnerable.* That is the central riddle of our doing God's reconciling work with God, for the reality of God is that in powerful sovereignty, God is revealed to be the poor person, the radically weak one who lords it over none (cf. Mark 10:42–44).

In the current, heated discussions about women in ministry, it is important not to lose sight of the redefinitions of power that may be offered to us in this struggle. It may be that God is calling the church to abandon hierarchial, coercive forms of power for the sake of vulnerable power that stands with and suffers alongside. We do not yet know what such power would mean, but clearly it means a sharp reorientation, for Jesus is judged by the world to be utterly powerless, and yet he did indeed have the only power that mattered.

Paul reflects on this riddle of power and vulnerability in 1 Cor. 1. He has discerned that the ways of the world (the Jew and the Greek) have the *forms of power* but have no *effective power* to hear, free, renew, or unite. It takes a very different kind of power to do that. It is power held not by the rich, the powerful, or those of noble birth, but only by those who are poor, lowly, and weak (1:26–28). That is the church that has ordered its life after the manner of Jesus himself, who had no power except the power of suffering solidarity that could change the lives of people.

If we were to embrace such a new orientation to power, then the notion of redistribution of power would not be so terrifying. The reconciliation among the peoples of our world concerns empowerment of the "little ones," the ones who never get to decide their own life. The task of reconciliation means to give such people economic and political freedom so that they may care for and have responsibility for themselves. Reconciliation is to give such people back their empowered personhood so that they may be fully engaged in the historical process.

3. Such a route to reconciliation means that *individual acts of compassion* are of little significance unless they are coupled with a *radical address to the public institutions* that shape our common life. The corporate structures of our society have inherent biases against people who do not qualify or meet certain standards. And of course, it is always the managers of the present arrangements who have set the standards. It has always been that way in human history. It was that way in the brickyards of Pharaoh. It was that way in the legalisms of narrow forms of Judaism in the time of Jesus. And it is so now, for the rules of the economic-political game define certain people as losers before they can even participate in the process. And there will not be reconciliation until that is overcome.

Reconciliation calls for disengagement from public institutions that are committed to enslaving and estranging persons. Or, said another way, reconciliation requires liberation. It cannot be a compassion that accepts existing institutional order, but it must call into question every order that produces slaves or orphans. The abrasiveness of Moses against the Egyptians' order, the challenge of the prophets against Israel's kings, the rejection of the public order of his day by Jesus, were premised on the conviction that public life can be for and not against the brothers and sisters. And sons and daughters must think anew of the divine dream to make their own this *odd mix of abrasiveness and vulnerability*. When sons and daughters think about that, they are driven to think about Jesus, who combined the *abrasiveness of dismantling* and the *vulnerability of solidarity* with people in their poverty and powerlessness. It is his cross that shows how power as the world knows it has no power, and the suffering way of solidarity has power just when the world thought Jesus was utterly without power.

4. Reconciliation concerns not only sisters and brothers but also the cypress and myrtles (Isa. 55:12–13), the lion and the lamb (Isa. 11:6–9). Reconciliation cannot countenance sisters and

brothers against each other. Similarly it cannot consider sisters and brothers against or in destructive tension with *God's good earth*. The daughters and sons who are heirs must take care of the parental estate. What is the point of being an heir unless there is something to inherit?

There is a long tradition that promises that the final hope of God's sons and daughters is to live face-to-face in the sacred presence. Eph. 1:3–10 anticipates the utter unity of the entire creation in the presence of God. That is promised to slaves and orphans who become God's children. And we are invited to live that dream, to live toward it and to be powered by it. We wait for that final moment of unity because we have confidence, already knowing who God is and what God is about. The Holy One is like the abrasive power and suffering vulnerability of Jesus of Nazareth. We already know who God is, for whoever has seen the child has seen the parent. In his *crucifixion of solidarity* with us and in his *resurrection of surprising newness,* we know two things. We know what is promised to us, because what Jesus has done is what Jesus will do. And we know what is asked of us, for we are called to share in his vision and work. And knowing those two things is enough. It is enough as a context in which we keep risky covenant with the utterly faithful one.

The vocation of the sons and daughters of this father is a demanding one. We grow weary and faint-hearted because it is more than can be done. It is at times impossible. That is how his disciples felt and how his church has often felt. But we have this enduring assurance: "For mortals it is impossible, but not for God; for God all things are possible" (Mark 10:27). And then Jesus states his salvific logic: "But many who are first will be last, and the last will be first" (Mark 10:31). That is finally how our reconciling work will be done. It is an end to all business as usual. But business as usual can end because God makes all things new. And in Jesus of Nazareth, we know it has begun among us. Hallelujah!

For Reflection and Discussion

1. Think about the images through which you understand yourself. (All of us use many such images.)
   - In what areas of your life do you function like a slave?
   - In what areas do you feel like an orphan?
   - What makes it possible for you to accept yourself as a trusted, loved child of God?
2. Of these three images, child, orphan, slave, which ones are reflected on television, which ones are taught in our schools?
   - Who are the slave owners?
   - Who runs the orphanage?
   - What about baptism as a way of adopting slaves and orphans to be children?
3. What kind of power does it take to become a child?
   - What power keeps people slaves or orphans?
   - What kinds of power are floating around in your experience?
4. The point of being a child is to be an heir.
   - What do you think you will inherit? from whom?
   - Do you have anxiety about being left out of the will?
   - What do you think God's last will and testament has in it for you?

Scripture Passages for Meditation

Luke 19:1–10
Rom. 8:14–25

Comment

Jesus had the remarkable capacity to speak and act so that people could be children of God. Luke, of all the Gospels, presents Jesus as concerned for the losers. Zacchaeus was surely an orphan, alienated from the family of God. He was up a tree in more ways than one. He was cut off from every hope. But the presence of Jesus made it possible for him to regain the family. Jesus affirms that the family promises are still for this man. He is heir to all the hopes of Abraham's family. And all the alienation couldn't void that. When God takes us as sons and daughters, we cannot deny it.

In Romans 8, Paul describes what it means to be God's child:

- to be able to name [God] and accept our life from [God] (v. 15)
- to be heirs and share in Christ's future (v. 17)
- to wait in patience (vv. 19, 25)
- to have glorious liberty (v. 21)
- to grow in heavy anticipation (v. 23)

Those are life agendas that are strange to outsiders but the source of life for insiders.

It might make a difference to think of church as the continuing family reunion where all the brothers and sisters remind one another of our inheritance, of being heirs to Jesus' suffering and glory. The church is always on the brink of forgetting who it is. Then it has no power. We are God's church when we grow with patience and eagerness.

9

The Bible
and Its Community

The preceding explorations have been based on an important presupposition: Bible study is not a neutral enterprise when it is faithfully done. It is not a matter of learning some data, historical or political, to be added to a store of general knowledge. It is not a matter of learning some theology that simply fits into a person's already existing believing apparatus. Bible study is not simply something someone does to the Bible. It is also something that has impact upon the interpreter. Serious Scripture study calls one to repentance and invites one to a changed perceptual world. Of course there is a danger of biblicism in such an approach. But our present danger is not that the Bible should be taken too seriously or given too much weight in our decision making. Rather the danger is that we miss its claim and fail to recognize its peculiar power and authority in the believing community.

The themes considered here, leading finally to repentance, death, and life, indicate a new consciousness to which we are called by the Scriptures. The Bible, of course, is not to be understood as being addressed primarily to individual persons. Rather it is to be understood as addressing the church, calling the church to its rightful identity and to its proper mission. The point of the Bible is "'to make ready a people prepared for the Lord'" (Luke 1:17).

We may observe that in the history of reform and renewal, return to the Scriptures has been recurringly a major moving factor.* Four examples may be noted:

1. In 2 Kings 22–23, *King Josiah* presides over a regime that is grossly syncretistic. The peculiar role of Israel and the particular understanding of the Lord, the God of Israel, have been eroded almost beyond recognition. But the narrative tells of a radical disengagement from those cultural forms and a radical reformation of the religious practice of the time.

Israel in the seventh century B.C.E. had become accommodated to the dominant cultural patterns of the period. This was evident in the easy terms with Assyrian power and authority. It also appeared in the embrace of Assyrian religious practices by the religious leaders of the realm. And it showed itself in syncretistic forms of worship and the neglect of matters of justice and human welfare. It is clear that Israel had ceded to Assyria the complete right to define the world in which it lived. No doubt there were many reasons for this, but clearly one was disregard for the tradition of faith expressed in the texts that subsequently became the Hebrew Scriptures. (Although this crisis technically comes before the formation of the Hebrew Scriptures, the role played by a venerated text tradition is closely paralleled to the later role of the Scriptures.) Israel and its king had forgotten who they were and had settled for other identities provided by alien voices. This was evident in religious practice, but it is clear that the inevitable result was the erosion of human values. The Torah serves to give religious identity as well as passion for justice. Both had disappeared in the time of Josiah.

Remarkably, when the scroll of the old tradition was found (commonly thought to be some form of the Book of Deuteronomy), Josiah and his realm were moved to radical repentance.

---

*On the power of Scripture in the Reformation of God's people, see the essay of my teacher, Allen G. Wehrli, "The Recurring Protestant Spirit," *The Heritage of the Reformation,* ed. Elmer J. F. Arndt (New York: Richard R. Smith, 1950), pp. 14–34.

Not only did he reform ritual activity, but he also directed social policy in new ways. The scroll served to call Josiah and Judah away from Assyrian presuppositions. Josiah embodies here the faithful community of God being led to repentance and renewal by the powerful voice of the Scriptures. He was amenable to that very old text (already very old in his time) and courageously reordered his life and office in terms of the text that had peculiar bite for him. The change wrought by the Scriptures was centered in a new seriousness about identity as God's peculiar and obedient people. The power of the text here is to reshape God's people. Taking the text seriously creates a radical change in historical reality.

2. In the sixteenth century C.E., we may note an important second example in the movement clustered around the name of *Martin Luther.* As in the time of Josiah, the community of faith in Luther's time had fallen into practices and perceptions clearly alien to the Gospel. That abuse was widely recognized not only by those who identified with Luther but also with those who resisted him, as in the case of Erasmus. The church had become enculturated and was less than fully faithful. It had become enmeshed in a consciousness of manipulative practice and mechanical modes that had nothing to do with the faith it confessed. A church that does not seriously engage in Scripture study runs a much graver risk of domestication.

No doubt there were many factors that led to that reform movement. Certainly Luther was not indifferent to the politics of the Reformation and the strain among the German princes in relation to the emperor. But at the center of the movement was Luther's preoccupation with Scripture and the drastic way in which the text was both the basis of radical criticism and the source of power for newness. The text tends to cut both ways, both to judge and renew, as it surely did in the Luther movement. Out of an attentive openness to the text powered by God's spirit, Luther was able to articulate a fresh discernment of who God is and what God's people are called to be. In so doing, he was able to call into question the presuppositions and values that tempted the church and that can only be described in terms of manipulation and fearful coercion. From the text Luther initiated a movement that did energize and reconstruct the church. It became not a personal crusade but a deep stir-ring among God's people that swept through the whole church, touching not only the newly structured "protestantism" but also the faithful church catholic. It is often not recognized that Luther's faith and action emerged after long and intense years of Scripture study.

3. Two centuries after the movement of Luther, we may note yet another parallel in the movement clustered around the name of *John Wesley*. Christianity in eighteenth century England had become arid and sterile in the extreme. It had no power and little credibility. In that period there were evidences of the stirring of God's people in various forms. Certainly John Wesley (no more than Luther) did not happen in a vacuum. There was in Wesley's period a context of evangelical expectancy.

Nonetheless, the sweep of the movement was both trig-gered and powered by Wesley's facing of Scripture. Scripture triggered it, for it was in the study of Scripture and its procla-mation that his heart "was strangely warmed." Scripture pow-ered the movement because there was never any doubt about its being simply a movement of self-improvement. The Wesley movement was intended to be a faithful embodiment of what had been given and learned in a study of Scripture. Like Luther, he paid central attention to Paul's letter to the Romans and was led there to discern a wholly fresh image of how God's people might be empowered to have life transformed. Out of that trig-gering came a vast movement that decisively influenced life in that period. His movement (now expressed in Methodism) has become a continuing testimony to God's renewing power. While the movement is surely a movement of God's spirit, it is important that the movement was shaped and initiated by Scripture. Without Scripture there might have been a movement of fervor, but only with Scripture is it powered by this peculiar memory and perspective that guards and sustains the church.

4. Among us we are most aware of the staggering reform of the church in *Vatican II*. Again we may note this shaping event did not happen in a vacuum. Long years of hoping and yearning had been combined with hard preparatory work on the part of those who could not see where it would lead but

who prepared in any case. Surely also the unique personhood of Pope John was a key trigger. But it is also sure that Vatican II had power and credibility because of the new ways in which Scripture had penetrated the mind and heart of the church.

The church in the pre–Vatican II period had apparently grown tired and lost much of its vitality. It did not seem to have the energy or courage to extricate itself from the place and role in culture into which it had fallen. The categories of its life and work were enmeshed in an intellectual and moral history in culture that largely immobilized it. But the careful, patient, and bold work of Scripture scholars and theologians had created a context for a renewal of faith and a deep embrace of a vocation under Jesus Christ.

A liturgical renewal opens up the resources of faith in ways that invite bold imagination, a new compassion for the hurts of the world, an openness and seriousness toward Jews as the people to whom God first and irrevocably gave "the adoption, the glory, the covenants, the giving of the law, the worship, and the promises" (Rom. 9:4; 11:29). The council in surprising ways has served to unfreeze the church, to open it to the leadership of God's spirit. It is too much to credit all of this to the Scriptures. But it is beyond any doubt that what happened did not and could not happen apart from the Scriptures. The precise connections are difficult to discern, but none will question its centrality for the new vitality in the church.

It is the function of the Scriptures to renew the church and call it to repentance. This repentance means to break off old ways. But repentance is also grounded in the bold promise of God that newness is to be given and new life is possible and more joyous. It is the nature of the church to be addressed, empowered, and called into question by the Scriptures. Scripture that does not move the church is likely Scripture not taken seriously. Church that is not powered by the Scriptures is likely not a faithful or powerful church. Each of the four examples we have cited, *Josiah* in the seventh century B.C.E., *Luther* in the sixteenth century C.E., *Wesley* in the eighteenth century, *Vatican II* in our time, presents a faith community that had lost its way and had been caught in the patterns and presuppositions of its cultural setting. Each reports an enmeshed community that is helpless in action and hopeless in faith. Each had become enamoured with other voices and had lost touch with the voice of God moving in the Scriptures. Each of these great reforms happened when the voice of God in the Scriptures broke through the enculturation and provided the church with a vision of its distinctiveness.

We must take care that the Bible is not treated as though it belonged only to the sphere of the church. The real issue before us now concerns not simply the church, its renewal, and its faithfulness, certainly not its well-being and effectiveness. God's agenda is not the church but *God's creation,* and to this Scripture is addressed. The call to repentance and the promise of new life is not only a gift announced to the church. It is God's purpose that all of creation, and surely the entire human community, should turn to God's service and joy. As the World Council of Churches has recently articulated, it is God's purpose that all creation should be *freed* and that it should be *united.* The Bible, if taken seriously, will not permit us to settle for a vision that is too narrowly focused on the church.

The question now before us, given the failure of so much that has been precious, is whether the "crisis of the human spirit" can be dealt with in ways that will heal, reconstruct, and renew. That crisis is evident on many fronts:

1. the isolation and alienation of persons
2. the failure of communities, even well-off communities, to care for their members
3. the disputes between haves and have-nots now so evident in the issues of energy and world hunger
4. the civil strife in so many places that devours brothers and sisters
5. the erosion of images and symbols that can heal and unite; we live our life and discern ourselves and our neighbors in ways that are sexist and racist
6. the insatiable consumerism that cheapens the life of us all

We live in a society where we nearly have forgotten what humanness is about. And that is why the Bible must be taken seriously. It preserves for us alternative images of humanness. It holds for us promises of a new age coming upon us. It bestows upon us, by the rule of God, power to become whom we are destined to be. We are offered "power to become children of God" (John 1:12) so that we may leave off being either slaves or orphans and we may stop building institutions to contain either slaves or orphans.

The Bible holds for us an invitation to another humanness. We need not be triumphalist. We need not always be securing ourselves at the expense of others. We need not regard ourselves as the last defense of what is right. It is enough that this notion of humanness in the image of God finds joy in caring, life in dying, strength in meekness. That is not commonly believed among us, even by those who use such words. But these affirmations have resilience and credibility among those who are not prepared to settle for current one-dimensional self-understanding. That is the issue around which our work must cluster. To that issue the Bible has a singular pertinence.

In the poor man Jesus of Nazareth, we have a new sense of our humanness. In his community we have a fresh discernment of being a distinct people in the history of the world, a people that lives always between the cost of Good Friday and the joy of Easter Sunday. The Bible insists upon our facing that call.

For Reflection and Discussion

1. In what ways do you discern "the crisis of the human spirit"?
2. What resources do you find for coping in liturgy? in prayer? in the Scriptures?
3. How much of your energy is used for coping, for keeping things as they are? How much of your energy is used for change, for being changed, for being renewed?
4. What in Vatican II has most provided hope and newness for you? What in Vatican II has most disappointed or angered you? What kind of newness do you most wish for the church? What kind of newness do you most fear for the church? How do these newnesses relate to the power and freedom of God?
5. What happens to your faith and life if repentance is understood as transformation?

Scripture Passages for Meditation

Isa. 55:6–9
Isa. 43:18–21
Eph. 4:17–24
Rev. 21:1–6

Comment

The central invitation of the Bible is to embrace newness. This newness comes from God and is possible because of who God is. It is newness that we cannot invent and most often we do not think it can happen. Most of us are heavily committed to what is old and exhausted, and we have quit hoping that God can do his newness among us.

Spend some time reflecting on the newnesses of God you do not think possible, or you do not want even if it is possible.

The two texts from Isaiah are from a time of exile. Israel was far from home, and freedom was hopeless. But this poetry talks about God's new way that will bring the people home. Reflect on the exiles around us and God's ability to deal with them.

The Ephesians text is probably a formula used at baptism. It invites and offers a "new personhood." What a promise! That we among us might reflect the fullness of God. We might ponder in new ways the future given us in baptism.

The text from Revelation is from a church under persecution from the Roman Empire. There seemed no future and all hope is crushed. Precisely in such times, the early church did its deepest hoping. It hoped not because things "seemed to be working out" but because God is Lord of our future.

All these texts in one way or another stand amazed and stunned by God's power to raise the dead. It remains for us to discern what among and within us is dead and where God is yet at work to begin a new history with us.

10

Summary:
Perspectives
on the Bible

The Bible continues to hold fascination for persons and for culture, though it may be variously understood or even totally misunderstood. Even those who understand very little about it tend not to be free of its compelling fascination. Indeed, in some quarters where it is understood least, fascination is keenest.

The preceding discussion presents a particular perspective on the Bible. It is not claimed that this is the only possible way of understanding the Bible, but it is urged that this perspective is both *faithful* to the character of the Bible and *energizing* for the faith and life of the church. Thus at the outset it is presumed that Scripture has to do with the *fidelity and vitality of the church*. Consequently, the perspective taken here leads to distinctive conclusions regarding each topic. That of course is the intent of the argument and the test of the perspective. Each perspective decisively shapes how the text is interpreted, and this perspective is no exception. Indeed, it is central to this discussion that it is this perspective more than any particular that is most important for handling the Bible. Not only should we pay careful attention to the *results* of Scripture study, but we should give great care to the *presuppositions*, for results are often already implicit in the presuppositions. Perhaps it would be as well, then, in this concluding chapter, to consider explicitly the presuppositions implicit in the perspective in this book.

1. This discussion has presumed that the Bible is a *present resource for faith* and not a historical curiosity. That seems rather obvious, but we should not underestimate the problems involved in such a judgment. It presumes that there is some significant impingement of these old texts upon the present and that there is a faithful community that stretches between the generations and binds the two together. Thus to say it is a present resource immediately characterizes the Bible as a book *in and for the believing community*—the Hebrew Scriptures for the Jewish people, these writings and those that make up what we call "the Christian Testament" for the Christian church, for only these communities together bind these old texts and the present.

This is not an external, formal judgment but a most important decision about the character of the Bible as being a *confessional statement* kept alive in a *confessing community* that by its very action announces the character of this book. Scholars have worked long and hard on saying just how this impingement may be understood, but we find this difficult to express. Most usually we simply do it in particular cases with particular materials without having an adequate theory for it. This may be the best that can be done at present.

But the alternative of mere historical curiosity is clearly to be rejected. The Bible is a strange book of odd literature with obscure images from alien cultures very different from our own. To some it seems archaic and primitive and therefore simply an object of historical investigation. It is surely clear that serious Bible study requires the best tools of historical and literary analysis, including archaeological and linguistic tools of a very technical kind. But the intent of such work, it is here insisted, is not to recover a museum piece as one might with an old Egyptian document that lies outside the confessing community. Rather the point is to *get inside the confessions and traditions* that can still be energizing for the church. The use of scholarly tools is to assist that process and not to impede it. To be sure, the materials have a "dated" character, but often encased in this is the raw passion of authentic faith as it shaped and guided the community. And this must not be missed because it is shaped and articulated in ways other than our own. That different shaping may provide us distance from our own practice of life and faith to help us discern the self-deception or self-serving that might characterize them.

2. The Bible is to be discerned *as much as a set of questions posed to the church as a set of answers.* The Bible provides an ultimate assurance to the issues of human history and destiny, the answer finally being that in God *self-giving graciousness* and *undoubted sovereignty* are identical. That is the central affirmation of the Bible that surely is an "answer" to the deepest questions of life. And nothing can detract from that.

But the Bible is often perverted when regarded as an answer book or a security blanket. This is evident in a most obvious way when the Bible is treated like a rabbit's foot or like a holy relic upon which to swear. But it is the same if the Bible is seen as a resolver of moral dilemmas or as a code for proper conduct. Such an approach attributes to the Bible a kind of static absoluteness that presumes the fixity of what is proper. It is the same when the Bible is seen as a collection of right doctrine that need only be "believed" without discerning its dynamic or historical character. These are all variations of the same theme, for each is an attempt to establish a norm beyond the demands and pressures of historical existence. The end result is to attribute to the Bible an absolute, unchanging quality (surely alien to its own evidence) that denies freedom to God and that denies our own historical responsibility.

The Bible finally is not concerned with right morality, right piety, or right doctrine. Rather it is concerned with *faithful relationships* between God and the people, between all the brothers and sisters in God's community, and between God's community and the world God has made. Faithful relationships of course can never be reduced to formulae but live always in the free, risking exchange that belongs to covenanting. It is this kind of exchange rather than fixed absolutes that is the stuff of biblical faith.

The central concerns of the Bible are not flat certitudes (even in the form of "eternal myths") but assurances that are characterized by risk and open mystery. The quality of certitude offered by the Bible is never that of a correct answer but rather of *a trusted memory, a dynamic image, a restless journey, a faithful voice.* Such assurances leave us restless and tentative in the relation, and always needing to decide afresh. Rather than closing out things in a settled resolution, they tend to open things out, always in fresh and deep question and urgent invitation. The central thrust of the Bible, then, is to raise new questions, to press exploration of new dimensions of fidelity, new spheres for trusting. Such questions serve as invitations to bolder, richer faithfulness. Such questions also serve as critics exposing our easy resolution, our faithless posturing, and our self-deception. If the Bible is only a settled answer, it will not reach us seriously. But it is also an open question that presses and urges and invites. For that reason the faithful community is never fully comfortable with the Bible and never has finally exhausted its gifts or honored its claims.

3. The Bible is not a statement of conclusions but *a statement of presuppositions*. To treat the Bible as though it "proves" things is both to misunderstand it and to judge it by alien processes. "Proof" always belongs to the realm of scientific verification, either by empirical or rational investigation. Either way, it consists in amassing data so that a conclusion is mandatory.

But this is not the characteristic way of the Bible, even though there are some forays into such a method. The characteristic logic of the Bible is confessional, assertive, and unargued. The Bible does not examine creation and conclude that God is creator. It does not review Israel's history and conclude that God redeems. It does not probe the history of the church and prove that Jesus has been raised. That is a form of knowing quite dominant among us in our mode of epistemology. But it is alien to the Bible.

The Bible *asserts* that God is creator and then draws derivative statements about creation. It *confesses* that God redeems and then asserts what this means for history. It *affirms* that Jesus is raised and then makes claims for the church. It operates in a very different universe of discourse that will not come to terms with the epistemology either of a doctrinally careful church nor with a scientifically oriented culture. It is curious that even some who have zeal for the authority of Scripture make the case in ways that concede other norms by which the Bible is tested rather than permitting the Bible its own assertive ground.

The faith premise of the Bible starts the other way around. The central substance of the Bible is not based in proof but in the courage and sureness of witnesses who dare bring testimony. And that testimony is in the posture of *confession, not proof.*

Few things so effectively deny power and vitality to the Bible as forcing it to meet other standards of knowing. The central substance of the Bible is *kerygma,* that is, proclamation that is never argued or demonstrated or proven, but only proclaimed as the bedrock of faith. Reading the Bible requires getting into that epistemology that is already an act of repentance, for it is prepared to believe the proclaiming voice without appeal to other norms. Thus acceptance of the "authority of Scripture" is not based on a formal assessment of the validity of a book but on a faith-decision to take as binding the voice of faith heard in the text. Such an assent of course does not ignore our ordinary experience, but without this initial assent there will be no serious facing of Scripture. It is urged here that the Bible is the beginning point and not the end result of faithful listening.

4. It is here presumed that the Bible is not an "object" for us to study but *a partner with whom we may dialog.** It is usual in our modern world to regard any "thing" as an object that will yield its secrets to us if we are diligent and discerning. And certainly this is true of a "book" that is finished, printed, bound and that we can buy, sell, shelve, and carry in a briefcase or place on a coffee table. Indeed we tend to do the same with persons, reducing them to objects so that they can be "read like a book."

Such a process reduces both the object and the subject. The one is passively acted upon; the other becomes an agent who acts in a unilateral way. Such a process violates the character of both parties, for in the image of God we are meant for the kind of dialog in which we are each time nurtured and called into question by the dialog partner—in this case, either by "book" or by person. Indeed, it is the task of Christian maturing

---

*See the discussion in Walter Brueggemann and Hans Walter Wolff, *The Vitality of the Old Testament Tradition* (Atlanta: John Knox Press, 1975), pp. 17–21, for a summary of two kinds of scholarship in relation to this question.

to become more fully dialogical, to be more fully available to and responsive to the dialog partner.

Reading the Bible requires that we abandon the subject-object way of perceiving things. It requires that we give up the notion of the Bible as a "book" to be acted upon, analyzed, studied, and interpreted. Perhaps it will help if we give up thinking of it as a "book" and regard it as a "tradition" that continues to be alive and surging among us. Such a change also requires that we give up our self-notion as subjects who come unilaterally to the text. This means that the text will continue to contain surprises for us, and conversely we discover that not only do we interpret the text but we in turn are interpreted by the text.

The position here assumed is that the Bible is not a closed object but a dialog partner whom we must address but who also takes us seriously. We may analyze, but we must also listen and expect to be addressed. We listen to have our identity given to us, our present way called into question, and our future promised to us.

5. The Bible has both a *central direction* and a *rich diversity*. Historical scholars tend to stress its diversity, and a serious reading must affirm this richness. This means that not all parts will cohere or agree. The Bible presents us with the treasure of many people in many times and places trying to live and believe faithfully. And we must take care that we are not *reductionist* because the richness staggers us and will not be contained in our best categories.

But theologians also stress the singularity of the Bible. It is, in a clear way, about one thing. There is "one faith, one baptism, one God and Father of all" (Eph. 4:5–6). Given certain differences, that oneness is characteristic of both the Hebrew Scriptures and the Christian Testament. And we must not *trivialize* the Bible by fragmenting it into many things in which we miss its central agenda.

We may not choose between these. It is like relating to a mature person in dialog. On the one hand there is a *rich unpredictability* of many resources that can be employed in many different ways. On the other hand, there is a *disciplined constancy* in which all experience coheres and has a single destiny.

It is like that with the Bible, and we must be open always to move in both directions with any given text.

6. The Bible is *a lens through which all of life is to be discerned.* No experience is seen in a vacuum but always through some set of experiences and some set of presuppositions. It is important that we become more knowing about various lenses that reflect interests and ideologies and decisively shape what we see.

The Bible is a special lens. It is radically different from every other perspective. It claims our perception at the most elemental levels. It calls into question every other way of seeing life. Thus at bottom the Bible invites us to a very different way of knowing, discerning, and deciding. A person who takes the Bible seriously is not one who takes simple answers from it or who memorizes a lot of Bible verses. Rather he or she is one who has had a changed consciousness because of the Bible's central affirmation of the *intersection of sovereignty and graciousness.*

All of this argues for the peculiar character and promise of the Bible that must be confessed and honored in all its power. The danger for serious Christians is that the Bible be domesticated and subordinated to other frames of reference. The explorations made in this study argue against such co-opting and insist that the Bible affirms a very different paradigm for humanness. Ever since the Exodus, the Bible has been asserting the rhetorical question:

"Who is like you, O LORD, among the gods?
    Who is like you, majestic in holiness,
    awesome in splendor, doing wonders?"

(Exod. 15:11)

The question is asked out of Israel's oldest, most radical confessional statement, the proclamation of the Exodus. It is that proclamation that determines the shape of the tradition.

The answer to the question is of course: None! Out of that comes a notion of our distinctiveness as God's children and God's people. It is cause for celebration and risk. It is also a point of entry for discerning what the Bible means to announce and what it promises to the faithful people.